One-Person Puppet Plays

Illinois Central College
Learning Resources Center

One-Person Puppet Plays

Denise Anton Wright

Illustrated by John Wright

TEACHER IDEAS PRESS
A Division of
Libraries Unlimited, Inc.
Englewood, Colorado
1990

TEACHER IDEAS PRESS
A Division of
Libraries Unlimited, Inc.
P.O. Box 3988
Englewood, CO 80155-3988

Library of Congress Cataloging-in-Publication Data

Wright, Denise Anton, 1958-
   One-person puppet plays / Denise Anton Wright ; illustrated by
John Wright.
    xiii, 236 p. 22x28 cm.
   Includes bibliographical references and index.
   ISBN 0-87287-742-6
   1. Puppet plays, American. 2. Puppet making. I. Title.
PN1970.W7 1990
812'.54--dc20   90-11030
                                     CIP

For John, my best audience,
with love

Contents

Preface xi

Acknowledgments xiii

Part 1
The Essentials of One-Person Puppet Plays

Introduction 3

The Puppets 4

Puppet Scripts 9

Puppet Stages 10

Props and Scenery 17

Puppet Manipulation 18

Puppet Voices 19

Your Audience 21

Presenting a Play 22

Follow-up Activities 23

Part 2
One-Person Puppet Scripts

Puppet Plays Adapted from Folklore and Fables. 27
   The Boy Who Cried Wolf. 27
   The Lion and the Mouse. 31
   The Town Mouse and the Country Mouse. 34
   The Johnny-cake. 41
   Sody Saleratus. 45
   Little Red Riding Hood. 52
   The Three Billy Goats Gruff. 58
   The Monkey and the Crocodile. 63

Puppet Plays with a Holiday or Seasonal Theme. 67
   Witch's Winter Kitchen. 67
   Why Cat Was Left Behind. 71
   Witch's Valentine. 76
   The Leprechaun's Gold. 80
   The Easter Egg Hunt. 85
   Easter Rabbit's Basket. 90
   The Back-to-School Blues. 96
   The Pumpkin Thief. 102
   Witch Gets Ready. 106
   The Halloween Costume. 109
   Turkey's Thanksgiving Adventure. 114
   Santa Cures a Cold. 118
   Santa's Reindeer. 124

Puppet Plays with an Emphasis on Reading and Libraries. 133
   The Case of the Disappearing Books. 133
   Monster Reads. 140
   Fox Learns a Lesson. 144
   Take Me to Your Library. 149
   Dragon Draws a Picture. 153

Puppet Plays Suitable for Any Occasion. 157
   The Dog Who Forgot. 157
   The Dragon Hunt. 161
   Elephant's Sneeze. 167
   The Mysterious Egg. 173

Part 3
Patterns for Puppets

Puppet Patterns. 181
   Paper-bag Mouth Puppets. 181
   Stick Puppets. 207
   Some Tips on Sewing Puppets. 214
   Finger Puppets. 214
      Details for Finger Puppets. 216

Mouth Puppets...216
    Details for Rounded-mouth Puppets...............................226
    Details for Pointed-mouth Puppets...............................226
Hand Puppets..227
    Details for Hand Puppets...230

Appendix A — Resources...231

Appendix B — Recommended Books on Puppetry...........................233

Preface

I want to share some background on how this book came about. Several years ago I assumed the position of children's librarian for a predominantly rural library system. As part of my job, I was expected to present programs in member school and public libraries. Often these audiences were composed of children ranging in age from two to ten years old. I realized the tremendous power puppets have to attract and hold the attention of a diverse audience, so I decided to include a short puppet play in every program I presented. Suddenly, I needed puppet scripts that one person could perform without too much difficulty, but finding them was another matter. I scoured the collections of local public and university libraries, publishers' catalogs, and catalogs of companies specializing in puppetry, but I wasn't satisfied with what I found. Either the published scripts required too many puppets, complex scenery changes, or numerous props (making them nearly impossible for one person to perform), or the scripts too strongly reflected another puppeteer's personality. Encouraged by several friends with backgrounds in puppetry, I drew upon my experience and training in theatre and began writing my own one-person puppet scripts. Finally, I was free to be my own playwright, director, and cast of characters, and I loved it!

This book is the result of those years writing scripts and presenting one-person puppet plays throughout central Illinois. Along the way, I developed my own philosophy concerning a simplified approach to puppet plays. That philosophy is presented here, along with the puppet scripts, in the hope that it might encourage you to make one-person puppet plays a part of your work with children. Above all else, have fun!

Acknowledgments

Thanks to Joanne Riley and Judy Nichols,
fellow librarians and storytellers, who first encouraged
me to write puppet scripts.

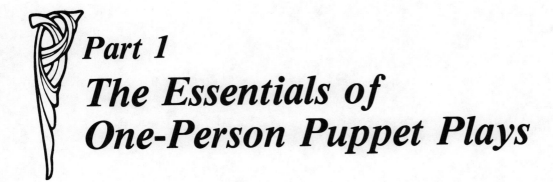

Part 1
The Essentials of
One-Person Puppet Plays

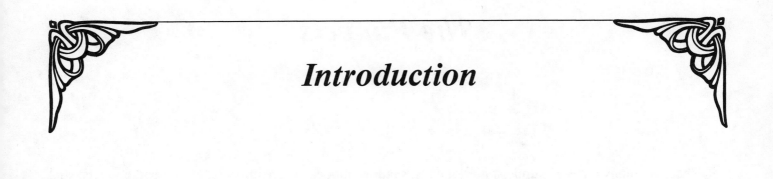

Introduction

During the past several years, while presenting one-person puppet plays in libraries, schools, and other settings, I've had teachers, librarians, day care providers, and parents tell me how much they enjoy puppets. Next they usually told me they would never be able to present puppet plays because they were not "professional puppeteers." Try as I might to encourage these people to attempt puppet plays, many of them remained convinced that only a "professional" can present puppet plays. Obviously, in the minds of many people, the term *puppet play* has come to mean an elaborate production, complete with lighting, scenery, costumes, and special effects—the kind of play that only a full-time professional would be able to present. This style of puppet presentation is magical and deserves its rightful place in contemporary puppetry. However, just as other art forms such as theatre, dance, and music have many different styles of presentation, so does puppetry.

As a librarian who works with young audiences, I wanted to use puppetry as a vehicle for storytelling and as a way to promote reading. To do this as a solo puppeteer traveling among a number of locations, I decided to pare my puppet plays down to only the essential elements. The success I have had with my one-person puppet style made me recognize the need for simplified plays an amateur puppeteer can present easily. I strongly believe that *anyone* is able to present entertaining and enlightening puppet plays for children. All it takes is an interest in puppetry and a desire to work hard at honing some basic puppetry skills. So now, let's examine the various components needed to present one-person puppet plays.

The Puppets

There are many types of puppets: marionettes, shadow puppets, glove puppets, mouth-rod puppets, stick puppets, finger puppets, and even full-body puppets. Although the scripts in this book can be performed with any of these types of puppets, I have discovered that four kinds are best suited for use in one-person puppet plays. For the purposes of this book, we will be discussing these four types: *glove puppets*, which include "mouth" puppets (Fig. 1) and "hand" puppets (Fig. 2), *finger puppets* (Fig. 3), and *stick puppets* (Fig. 4). All four types can be manipulated with only one hand, thus enabling one puppeteer to use two puppets simultaneously.

Simple directions on how to make these four basic types of puppets are included in part 3, Patterns for Puppets. Also, the list of recommended books on puppetry in appendix B suggests some excellent books which include puppet patterns. If you do not care to create your own puppets, there are many companies which produce high-quality puppets at fairly reasonable prices. Luckily, more and more retail stores now carry puppets as a regular part of their merchandise. Applause, Dakin, Folkmanis, and Russ are four of the large puppet manufacturers who sell primarily to retail stores. Some places to look for puppets are large department stores, children's specialty shops, and school supply stores. The resources in appendix A of this book include the addresses of several puppet manufacturers who will sell directly to individuals or to nonprofit organizations.

If you want to begin presenting puppet plays but do not have access to any puppets, it is not necessary immediately to purchase or create dozens of puppets in order to use the scripts found in this book. I have purposely kept the number of different puppet characters required in these plays to a minimum. When I first began presenting puppet plays, I had a very limited number of puppets available for use, and the majority of these were of various animal characters. As a result, the scripts I wrote revolved around these available puppet characters. Bit by bit, as my budget for puppets increased, so did the variety of my collection of puppets. Even with a larger array of puppets available, though, I still find myself relying on the same handful of characters I have used in the past. I discovered that these familiar puppets have become my old friends; I know their personalities, voices, and general behavior. Likewise, my audiences have also grown very attached to these characters. Because I often present a series of programs in a specific library, children will request a favorite puppet character for the next puppet play.

With the scripts in this book, I have also tried to write broad character "types" rather than specific characters. Because it is a character type, an evil Fox can just as easily be portrayed by a Troll, an Alligator, a Monster, or a Dragon. Naturally, there will be occasions when a specific character (such as Johnny-cake or Troll) is required in the script. In these cases, part 3, Patterns for Puppets, should come in handy. For the most part, though, try to think about broad character types when reading each of the puppet scripts.

(Text continues on page 9.)

4

Fig. 1. Mouth puppet

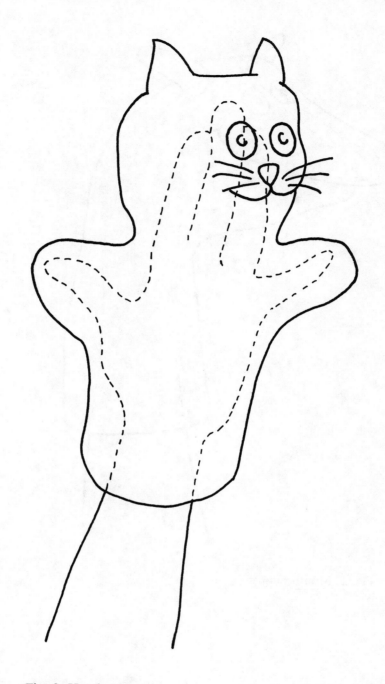

Fig. 2. Hand puppet

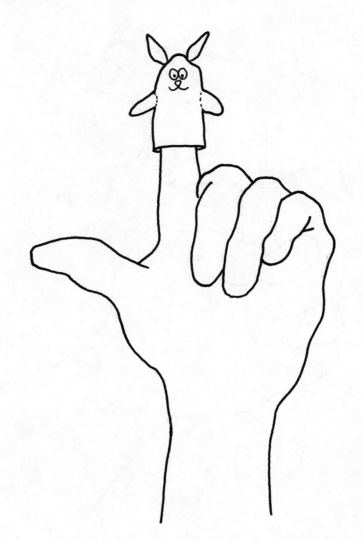

Fig. 3. Finger puppet

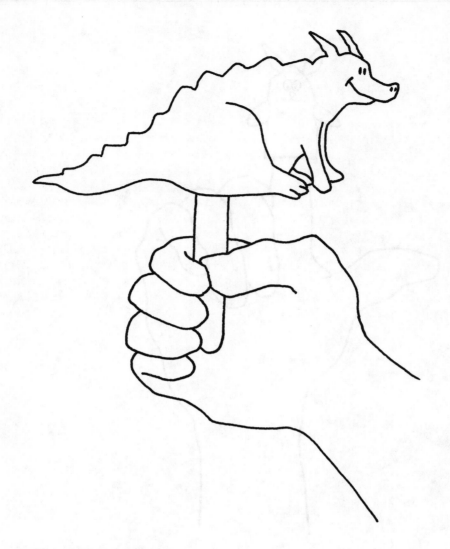

Fig. 4. Stick puppet

Puppet Scripts

Each of the thirty puppet scripts contained in this book can be presented in roughly ten to twenty minutes. Because they were written to be performed by only one person, no more than two puppets appear onstage at any one time (the only exception to this occurs in "Sody Saleratus," in which one puppet character holds an empty puppet from which a series of other puppet characters "emerge"). For each script, I have included what I feel to be essential stage directions, character motivation, and broad guidelines for puppet characterization. Occasionally, I have added a "Note" to the puppeteer at the beginning of a script in order to clarify the origin or my adaptation of a play. As you read through these scripts, try reading them aloud; these scripts, like all plays, were written to be spoken. Please don't regard these scripts as carved in stone. They are only intended to be guidelines for your puppet plays. If my sense of timing and dialogue agrees with you, that's great, but feel free to personalize the scripts by having the characters speak or move in a manner that makes sense to you. Even though all these scripts were written with one puppeteer in mind, they also work well when presented by two puppeteers.

Puppet Stages

To present a puppet play, you do not necessarily need to use a stage. Children have such a strong belief in the "realness" of puppets that, while watching a puppet play presented without a stage, they soon ignore the puppeteer and concentrate on the puppet characters. Presenting a puppet play without a stage creates an informal, relaxed atmosphere and allows for more puppeteer-audience interaction. Try presenting one of the simpler scripts in this book without a puppet stage and see what you think; you might just prefer this method of presentation. Personally, I have always felt more comfortable using a stage simply because it allows me to better concentrate upon puppet manipulation, voices, and the story line of the play. Disappearing behind a stage also feeds my love of the theatrical—that "putting on a play" feeling. One of the major disadvantages of presenting puppet plays with a stage is that it becomes nearly impossible to keep a close watch on your audience. For this reason, I always ask a responsible adult to monitor the audience during a play just in case any unexpected emergencies arise.

For those who prefer presenting puppet plays with the help of a stage, here are four types of stages which are well-suited for one-person puppet plays. They are all fairly easy to construct, are portable to varying degrees, and can be transported and stored. The first type is the *table-top proscenium* stage (Figs. 5a, 5b, and 5c). This is the type of stage I use most often, and I feel it is ideal when presenting one-person puppet plays. It is very portable, fits into the trunk of most cars, can be set up in just a few minutes, and is lightweight enough to save wear and tear on the puppeteer. Three views of this table-top stage are given in case you should want to construct your own. Figure 5a is the front view of this stage as the audience sees it. Figure 5b is the back view as the puppeteer sees it, and Figure 5c is the same front view with actual dimensions. The table-top proscenium stage consists of three panels: a wide middle panel and two narrower side panels. Each panel is constructed by covering a wood frame with fabric (canvas, heavy burlap, or even polyester work well). These panels are then hinged together to allow for ease in folding and transporting. The wide middle panel contains the proscenium opening for the puppet performance area. A narrow board can be hinged to the audience-side lower edge of this proscenium opening, making a simple shelf which then becomes the "floor" of the stage for the puppets. This shelf comes in handy when puppets need to set prop items on their portion of the stage.

Approximately six to eight inches behind the middle panel rests the curtain of this style of puppet stage. A lightweight cotton or cotton/polyester-blend fabric works well for the curtain, which is cut double the width of the proscenium opening and then gathered over a narrow curtain rod. An extendable cafe curtain rod works best for this purpose. A large screw eye attached to the upper wood frame of each side panel holds either end of this curtain rod in place. With this table-top proscenium puppet stage, the puppeteer may either kneel or sit behind the stage during the puppet play. The table this type of stage rests on should always be covered with a large tablecloth or sheet before the stage is set up.

A variation of the table-top proscenium stage is the *standing proscenium* puppet stage (Fig. 6a). As its name implies, this type of stage rests on the floor rather than on the top of a table and is used by a puppeteer standing behind it during the play. This stage can be constructed to any height, but most standing proscenium stages tend to be six feet tall. Figure 6a is the front view of this stage, as the audience sees it, while Figure 6b is the back view, as seen by the puppeteer. The middle panel remains the same as for the table-top proscenium stage but, because of its increased height, each of the two side panels needs to be at least three-quarters the width of the middle panel. The proscenium opening, curtain, curtain rod, and shelf remain the same as in the table-top proscenium stage. You will notice that Figure 6b shows an added feature which the table-top version lacks. This is the "prop shelf," a narrow board hinged approximately twelve inches below the lower edge of the

(Text continues on page 15.)

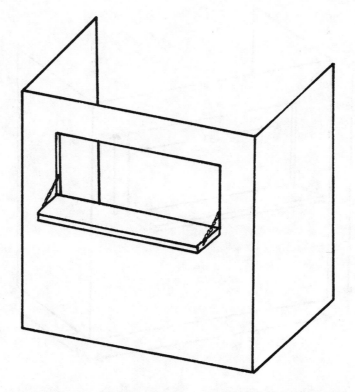

Fig. 5a. Table-top proscenium puppet stage (front)

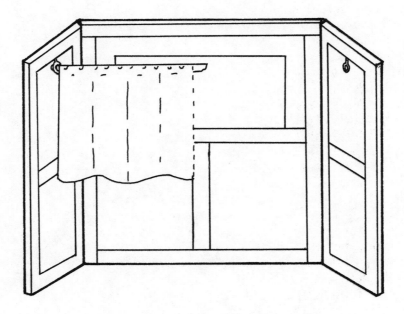

Fig. 5b. Table-top proscenium puppet stage (back)

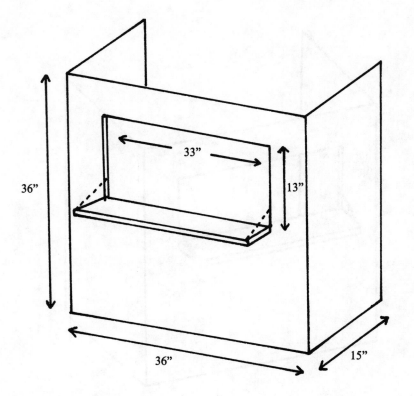

Fig. 5c. Table-top proscenium puppet stage (front)

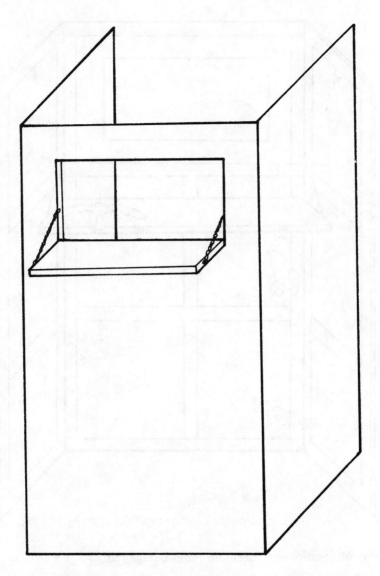

Fig. 6a. Standing proscenium puppet stage (front)

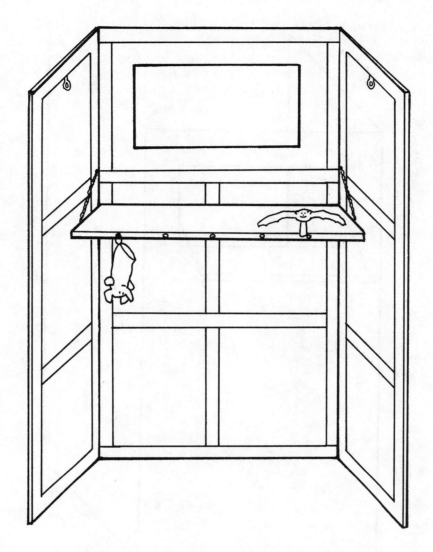

Fig. 6b. Standing proscenium puppet stage (back)

proscenium performance area. The construction of this shelf is almost identical to that of the shelf forming the bottom of the proscenium performance area or stage floor. This prop shelf is ideal for storing prop items which are not needed onstage, and also allows the puppeteer to hang unused puppets by small cup hooks screwed into the edge of the shelf. A small plastic ring sewn into the lower hem of the puppet allows the puppet to hang from the cup hook. Because of its larger size, the standing proscenium stage is heavier and bulkier than the smaller table-top version; thus, it is not as portable. This stage can still be folded for easy storage, and has the advantage of not requiring a table.

A related version of the standing proscenium stage is the *standing screen* puppet stage (Fig. 7). This is a simpler version, consisting merely of three panels hinged together. The wide middle panel in this version does not have a proscenium opening as a performance area; instead, the puppets simply appear at the top of the middle or side panels. As with the standing proscenium stage, the puppeteer stands behind the stage during the play. This type of stage can be constructed so that the hinges holding the panels together have removeable pins, which allows the panels to come apart for ease in transportation and storage.

The fourth and last type of puppet stage is the *doorway* stage (Fig. 8). It is the simplest stage to construct and is simply a length of fabric gathered over a tension rod and placed across a doorway. The height of this stage depends on whether a child or adult will use it. Because of its simplicity, this type of stage is ideal for informal puppet plays with children. As with the standing screen puppet stage, the puppets perform at the top of this stage.

These are just four of the simplest types of puppet stages. The list of recommended books on puppetry in appendix B contains several books and booklets which suggest other styles and types of puppet stages. Also, appendix A includes the address of a company that has several puppet stages available for purchase.

Fig. 7. Standing screen puppet stage

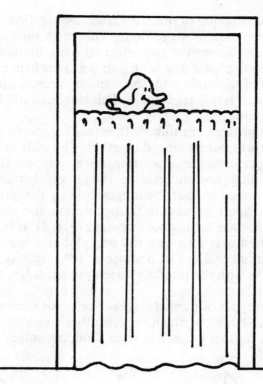

Fig. 8. Doorway puppet stage

Props and Scenery

If you are presenting a puppet play by yourself, the last thing you need is to battle with too many props. That is why props are used only when absolutely necessary in these scripts. Required props are listed at the beginning of each script directly following the cast of characters. One thing to keep in mind when reading the scripts is that the props do not always need to be the actual item. For example, Witch's broom can be either a miniature broom or a cardboard cut-out of a broom. Cardboard cut-outs may also be used for several other prop items such as a basket, pot of gold, or a pumpkin. When actual props are needed for these scripts, they can usually be purchased in a craft store or toy department or easily made at home.

Even though few props are needed in these scripts, they still require careful manipulation. The props for these scripts fall into two general categories: those which the puppeteer puts on the puppet (such as a hat, a bandage, a net, or a ghost costume) and those which seem to the audience to be manipulated by the puppet. Occasionally, a puppet is actually able to do all the necessary prop manipulation, but most often it is a combination of the puppet *and* the puppeteer manipulating a prop. A major influence upon the manipulation of props is whether you are using a puppet stage for presenting the play. The proscenium stages discussed previously in this part (Figs. 5a, b, and c and 6a and b) feature an optional shelf that is ideal when puppets need to set something onstage (such as Leprechaun and his pot of gold, Easter Rabbit and his basket, or Witch and her cauldron). This proscenium stage is also ideal when using a cardboard cut-out rather than the actual item. When a puppet needs to set a cardboard prop onstage, small pieces of Velcro firmly glued to both the cut-out and the inside bottom opening of the proscenium part of the stage assure a secure hold.

There are other times when a prop becomes almost another character in the play. For example, in *Witch Gets Ready*, Witch's broom seems to have a mind of its own as it moves about the stage. This is one of the few times when the puppeteer alone controls the manipulation of a prop. To give the illusion of a puppet manipulating a prop, the puppeteer often needs to help hold or move the prop from below the stage, unseen by the audience. Extra rehearsal time and practice is always needed whenever puppets and props come together, but the results are worth it.

Scenery is not required to present any of the scripts included in this book. Naturally, if you want to add scenery or stage pieces to your puppet plays, feel free. For basic shapes or forms, such as a bridge for Troll in *The Three Billy Goats Gruff* or a tree for Monkey in *The Monkey and the Crocodile*, a cardboard cut-out works well. Use a procedure similar to that mentioned earlier for cardboard cut-out prop items. Simple scenery or set pieces may be attached to the bottom or sides of the proscenium performance area of the puppet stage with Velcro.

Puppet Manipulation

Luckily, the types of puppets which are best suited for use in one-person puppet plays (mouth, hand, finger, and stick puppets) are all fairly easy to manipulate. Most mouth puppets are manipulated by the puppeteer slipping a hand into the puppet and then moving the thumb away from the palm of the hand (see Fig. 1 in the preceding discussion). This movement gives the impression of the puppet "talking," but mouth puppets are capable of even more movements. They are able to make a sour or perplexed expression by the puppeteer curling the fingers inside the puppet, and are able to bend, stretch, or nod with a flick of the puppeteer's wrist.

Hand puppets afford the puppeteer a wider variety of manipulating positions, but the first procedure is for the puppeteer to slip a hand into the puppet with the fingers and thumb placed into the two "hands" of the puppet and its head. Some puppeteers use the thumb and little finger as the puppet's "hands," leaving the remaining three fingers to act as the puppet's head (see Fig. 2 in the preceding discussion). Other puppeteers use the thumb and either the last two or three fingers as the puppet's "hands," with the middle and/or index finger manipulating its head. Whichever position you choose, it is hardly a natural one for your hand; as a result, a great deal of practice is necessary to make hand puppets move in a realistic way. Simple hand puppets do not have moveable mouths, and so the puppeteer must provide the illusion of the puppet "talking" through a gentle nodding or sideways movement of its head and body. Hand puppets are able to use their "hands" expressively to clap, point, scratch, hit, or pick up and hold objects. Like mouth puppets, hand puppets are also able to bend, scretch, or twist with a movement of the puppeteer's wrist.

Finger puppets are manipulated by the puppeteer inserting a finger, usually the index finger, into the puppet (see Fig. 3 in the preceding discussion). The movements of finger puppets are fairly limited, but they can nod, shake, twist, or bend by the puppeteer moving the finger slightly. As with hand puppets, the absence of moveable mouths means that finger puppets must create the illusion of talking by slightly moving their bodies.

Stick puppets are manipulated by the puppeteer simply holding onto the stick, rod, or straw attached to the puppet character (see Fig. 4 in the preceding discussion). Possibilities for stick puppet movements are limited to such broad motions as walking, hopping, or skipping.

When practicing puppet manipulation, it is best for the puppeteer to work in front of a mirror. This way, the actual movements of the puppet can be clearly observed. Keep in mind that every movement the puppet makes should be meaningful. Movement without a reason or motive becomes very distracting for your audience. To make movements more meaningful, try practicing a variety of exercises with the puppet. How would the puppet move if it were angry? Hurt? Frustrated? Happy? Frightened? Cajoling? Sleepy? Tired? Depressed? The list of possible feelings and motivations goes on and on. Think of the puppet as an actor, with you its director as well as its way of coming to life. Remember, the puppet is only able to do what *you* make it do, so practice, practice, practice! An excellent source of practical manipulation exercises is *Making Puppets Come Alive* by Larry Engler and Carol Fijan, listed in appendix B of this book.

Manipulating any type of puppet requires the puppeteer to place hands and arms in unnatural positions. This is especially true when presenting puppet plays from behind a stage. In order for the puppet to appear in the proscenium opening of a stage or at the top of a screen the puppeteer must hold his or her arms at right angles or raised above the head for extended periods. With arms in this position, the puppeteer may find even the shortest puppet play seems as if it goes on for hours! Several things will help this fatigue: if you aren't accustomed to holding your arms in these positions, start off presenting puppet plays where one character has most of the time onstage. This way you can get one arm at a time used to presenting puppet plays. Also, if you haven't presented plays from behind a stage in a while, don't begin by doing a very long play. It's much easier to tackle a short play and then slowly work on increasing your endurance.

Puppet Voices

One of the reasons I have tried to limit the number of puppets needed in these scripts is that, with fewer puppets to manipulate, voices for those puppets become much easier for the puppeteer to provide. I believe that, lurking inside every would-be puppeteer, there is a wide variety of voices. The trick is becoming comfortable enough to let them out. This is one instance in which presenting puppet plays from behind a stage is helpful. The anonymity a stage provides is ideal for experimenting with voices you would never dream of making in *front* of a stage.

After reading through a puppet script several times, think about the characters. What sort of voice would fit each character? Would the character have a deep, resonant voice? Or maybe a high-pitched, squeaking voice? Also, keep in mind the rate at which each character speaks. When thinking about possible voices for puppets, don't forget your own. I have always found it helpful to give one character in every puppet play I present a voice very similar to my own. That puppet may speak faster or slower than I normally do, but I still recognize it as my comfortable, day-to-day voice. This way, there is one puppet's voice which comes naturally to me — a voice I don't have to strain to remember. Then, depending on how many other characters there are, I use a deeper or a higher voice for each puppet. This range of voices not only provides a good contrast for your audience but makes it easier for you to remember the voices. Since I use so many of the same puppet characters repeatedly in my scripts, I find it helpful to keep notes for myself concerning their voices. Also, I usually create a mental picture of that character to use while performing the play. That way, after enough practice, when I think "Witch," her voice just naturally comes forth. As with any performance situation, I occasionally make a blunder — I fail to change voices for a change in characters or even forget what the voice of an earlier character was like. When this happens to you (and chances are that it just might), relax and forget about that mistake. In most cases, your audience members didn't notice and probably wouldn't mind even if they had. The important thing is not to let that one little mistake ruin your entire puppet play.

Now is a good time to discuss the "live" or "taped" schools of thought in puppet play presentation. Many puppeteers prefer to audiotape their plays for a more accomplished performance. With a taped play, the puppeteer is able to add music, sound effects, and a wide array of vocal characterizations. In order to produce a good quality tape, you must naturally use excellent equipment for both recording and playback. If you choose to use a taped format for your puppet play, keep in mind that the unexpected sometimes happens — tapes foul and equipment jams. Therefore, it's a good idea to be prepared for any emergency by knowing the script yourself and having worked on voices and puppet characterizations.

Taping a play definitely adds more dimensions to the puppet performance, and taped music is ideal to suggest shifts in setting or time, but, for one-person puppet plays, I have always preferred to use a live format. I enjoy portraying the characters at the moment the audience is seeing them, and I find it is easier to keep my train of thought on the story line of the play. There are also a few practical considerations to recommend live productions. If your audience is unruly or even overly enthusiastic, it is comforting to have the option of a puppet character quieting them down and keeping control over the situation. Whenever a puppet makes use of a prop, there is always the possibility of that prop falling, flying, or failing to work properly. When things like this have gone awry, I have even had puppets ask that an audience member return a prop which has landed in the audience. Also, there is always the outside chance that a puppet play is "bombing" with a particular audience and mercifully needs to be shortened or condensed. Whatever your individual preference, please experiment with both formats and discover which suits your needs best.

One of the disadvantages of live productions is that, besides creating the voices for your puppets, you must also create any necessary sound effects. For that reason, you will find few sound effects in these scripts. One that appears occasionally, however; is the "knock at the door." To achieve this effect, simply tap your elbow against the top of a table if you are using a table-top stage. If you are using a standing stage, simply stamp your foot on the floor. Any other sounds effects, such as sneezing, snoring, making different animal sounds, or singing, should be fairly easy to accomplish. Just remember that your sound effects—and the voices you use—need to be heard by all members of your audience, so practice projecting your voice until this is possible without straining your voice.

Your Audience

I cannot stress enough how important it is always to consider your audience when selecting a puppet script for presentation. It is vital to choose the right script for the right audience. The scripts included in this book were written for use with audiences approximately two to nine years in age. While all these scripts can be appreciated to some degree by all ages, some are better suited for preschoolers and others to school-age audiences. Preschoolers respond well to plays with easily recognizable characters, lots of repetition, visual jokes, and aspects of audience participation. School-age children are able to appreciate more complex plots and a wider range of humor. I purposely avoided labeling these scripts with designated age levels because an audience's readiness to appreciate any puppet play is a very personal and subjective matter. You know the interests and needs of your audience better than I possibly could, so I leave the final selection to you.

I usually say the age of nine is the time when children become a restless audience for puppet plays. At this age, children are more interested in becoming the puppeteer than in being the audience, so it's the perfect opportunity to let them do just that—become the puppeteer! Workshops that allow children to construct puppets and present their own plays are ideal for this transitional time. If you're looking for scripts to use with the children, why not try some of the ones in this book? Many of them have been successfully presented by older children in this type of workshop situation. The list of recommended books on puppetry in appendix B offers some ideas for excellent sources on presenting puppet construction workshops with children. Also, part 3 includes simple puppets which older children can easily construct and use in their plays.

Presenting a Play

Now that you have puppets, an appropriate script, a stage, props, and voices for the puppets, what next? How do you actually go about presenting a puppet play? The first consideration is the setting or environment where your puppet play is to be presented. Presenting a puppet play in a library setting is a very different experience from presenting one in a shopping mall. If possible, have your puppet stage or performance area prepared before your audience arrives. Make certain that your area is out of high-traffic areas, away from doors that will be constantly opening and closing, and removed (if possible) from any distractions. Your aim is to have your puppet play be the focus of attention, so do everything possible to achieve this.

If your puppet play is part of a longer program, you may want to save the play for last. Children respond enthusiastically to puppets, so it is best to end your program on a high note. Before the puppet play begins and when your audience is sitting comfortably, let them know how you expect them to behave during a play. This does not have to be done in a scolding or preachy fashion; there are many entertaining ways of doing it. I often use a large animal "mascot" puppet to demonstrate the importance of listening, watching, and being quiet while the puppets are onstage. If you would like participation from your audience at some point during the play, prepare them now by asking for their help. When dealing with young audiences, I also tell them a little about the story of the play, without, of course, spoiling the ending. Then, with your audience settled and with excitement in the air, begin your puppet play.

When using a puppet stage, I always prefer being honest with my audience and telling them that I am going behind the stage to manipulate the puppets. With young children, I usually phrase it as "helping" the puppets—which, in actuality, is what happens.

Once you are behind the stage, it is a good idea to have a copy of your puppet script handy. If the script is fairly new to you or somewhat complex, it is useful to refer to the script while presenting the play. With a table-top stage, the puppets, props, and script can lie easily on the table, waiting for the puppeteer to use them. A standing-style stage poses a few more challenges in access to these items. That is why most standing stages possess a prop shelf under the performance area. This shelf can hold props while they are not needed onstage, can be used to store puppets, and can also accommodate a script.

By thoroughly rehearsing a play, with the stage, props, and puppets you will be using during your puppet presentation, many of the problems which might possibly arise are eliminated. This rehearsal period is when you iron out entrances, exits, prop manipulation, pacing, and stage business. Once a play is finished, it is a good idea for the puppeteer to come from behind the stage and talk to the audience. It is the perfect chance to pass out coloring sheets and other follow-up activities and to answer any questions your audience may have concerning the puppet play. If children ask to see the puppets or to look behind the stage, I normally discourage them by telling them that the puppets have finished their performance for the day and should be allowed to rest. I feel that children need to learn the distinction between a puppet performance and the more informal opportunities for behind-the-scenes workshops and tours.

Follow-up Activities

I always like to give my audience something to take home concerning the puppet play they have just experienced. This reinforces the story of the puppet play and continues the good memories of the occasion. The "something" can be a coloring sheet or a bookmark featuring the characters from the play, or a take-home pattern for a paper bag or stick puppet. This does not need to be elaborate or take hours of preparation time. The illustrations accompanying these puppet scripts can be photocopied as they are, or enlarged to become coloring sheets. These illustrations can also be reduced on a photocopier and made into the format of a bookmark. Part 3 contains several patterns for simple paper-bag and stick puppets that can be constructed by even young children. Besides being a take-home activity, these simple patterns also make a fun group activity following the puppet play. By using paper-bag or stick puppets, children can then present their very own puppet plays for friends and family.

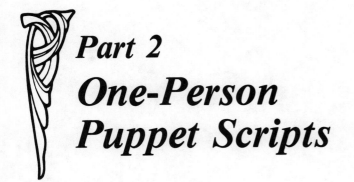

Part 2
One-Person Puppet Scripts

Puppet Plays Adapted from Folklore and Fables

THE BOY WHO CRIED WOLF

CHARACTERS: Boy (easily bored and wanting some excitement in his life)
Lamb (an animal under the boy's care)
Man (a townsperson who comes to help the boy)
Wolf (a bumbling animal who is also easily bored)

(BOY and LAMB enter the stage. LAMB is contentedly grazing while BOY is anxiously pacing back and forth across the stage, sighing loudly.)

BOY: (to the audience) Gosh, is this ever a boring job! All I do all day long is watch this dumb old lamb! There's nothing to do up here on this mountain. It's boring, boring, boring! I could be playing with my friends right now if it weren't for this boring old lamb!

LAMB: (disagreeing with BOY) Baaaa!

BOY: (to the audience) You know, lambs have to be the most boring animals in the whole world! All they ever do is eat and sleep ... eat and sleep! (to LAMB) I wish a wolf would come along and eat you up, you dumb old lamb!

LAMB: (angrily) Baaaa!

(LAMB exits the stage in a huff.)

BOY: (calling offstage after LAMB) Go ahead and leave! See if I care! You'll be back. (to the audience) Gosh, it sure would be exciting if a wolf *did* come along. I've got an idea! I'm going to pretend there's a wolf right here! That will stir things up a bit. I'm going to start yelling right now: "Help, help! It's a wolf! A wolf is here and he's going to eat me! Quick, somebody help me!"

(MAN runs onstage, very excited.)

MAN: (to BOY) What's the matter? Are you hurt? Where is the wolf?

BOY: (innocently) Gosh, I guess all that yelling scared the wolf away.

MAN: Well, the main thing is that you're safe. If that wolf comes back, you just start yelling and I'll run up here and help you.

(MAN exits the stage.)

BOY: (to the audience) That sure was fun! That was so much fun that I think I'll do it again. I'm going to scream and yell and pretend there's a wolf right here: "Help, help! It's a wolf! A wolf is here and he's going to eat me! Quick, somebody help me!"

(MAN runs onstage, a little slower than the first time but still very excited.)

MAN: (out of breath) What's the matter? Where's the wolf? (looking around the stage) I don't see any wolf here. (suspiciously) Are you sure there was a wolf here?

BOY: (sweetly) The wolf was right here. I guess my yelling scared him away.

MAN: (still suspicious) Well … I'll be down at the bottom of the mountain in case that wolf comes back.

(MAN exits the stage.)

BOY: (to the audience) This is really fun! I don't know why I never thought about this before! I just love getting all this attention. I think I'll try it one more time. I'm going to scream and yell and pretend there's a wolf right here: "Help, help! It's a wolf! A wolf is here and he's going to eat me! Quick, somebody help me!"

(MAN runs onstage, very slowly. He is barely able to breathe.)

MAN: (exhausted) Okay, now where is that wolf? I don't see any wolf here. (angrily) I think you're making all this up! I'm going back down the mountain and I'm not coming back up here for any reason. Do you understand?

(MAN angrily exists the stage.)

BOY: (to the audience) Gosh, he sure is mad. Some people are so grouchy! Nobody wants me to have any fun! (looks around the stage) Where did that dumb old lamb wander off to? I'd better go find him otherwise I'll be in even *more* trouble.

(BOY exits the stage. Soon WOLF enters the stage, looks around the stage, and sighs loudly. WOLF is obviously very bored.)

WOLF: (to the audience) I am *so* bored! There's nothing to do. (looking offstage) Wait! What's that over there? It looks like a boy. I've got a great idea. I'm going to scare the daylights out of that boy. Won't that be fun? I'll just hide right over there.

(WOLF crouches to one side of the stage. BOY enters the stage from the opposite side.)

BOY: (to the audience) I can't find that lamb anywhere. Now I'm really going to be in trouble!

(WOLF jumps out from his hiding place and does his best to scare BOY.)

WOLF: Grrrr.

BOY: (terrified) Oh no! It's a wolf! Help, help! A wolf! A wolf is here and he's going to eat me! Quick, somebody help me! Help! There *really* is a wolf here. Please help me! (to WOLF) You'd better not come any closer, or I'll scream!

(BOY runs offstage, still screaming for help.)

WOLF: (to the audience) Did you see that boy run? Gee, that sure was fun! I think maybe I should run after him and scare him some more.

LAMB: (from offstage) Baaaa!

(WOLF is just about to exit the stage but hears LAMB and stops.)

WOLF: (frightened) What was that noise? It sounded like a lamb!

(LAMB enters the stage from the opposite side.)

WOLF: (terrified) Oh no! It's a lamb! Help me, I'm afraid of lambs!

LAMB: (trying to calm WOLF) Baaaa!

WOLF: (to LAMB) Don't you come any closer, or I'll scream!

(WOLF runs offstage, still screaming for help.)

LAMB: (to the audience) Baaaa! I never knew wolves could be scared so easily. That was fun! Goodbye, everybody.

(LAMB exits the stage.)

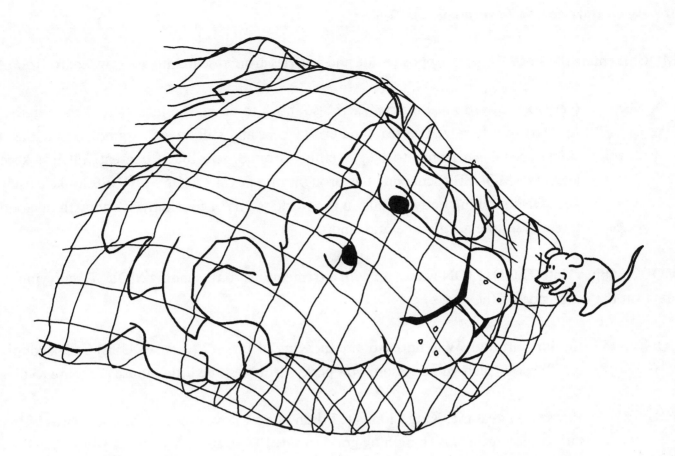

THE LION AND THE MOUSE

CHARACTERS: Lion (the haughty King of Beasts)
                         Mouse (a humble creature searching for food)

PROPS: A net to be thrown over Lion (which can be made by knotting together several pieces of string or cord).

(LION strides onstage.)

LION: (to the audience) Hello. I'm so glad you could all be here today. Of course you know who I am. Everybody knows Lion, the King of Beasts! Just to give you an idea of what I can do, here is one of my favorite roars. (LION lets out a mighty roar.) Would you like to hear another one? (LION waits for a response from the audience, then lets out with another mighty roar.) Whew, all this roaring has tired me. I think I'll lie down right here and take a short nap—a "cat" nap, you might say. (LION laughs heartily at his own feeble joke and then settles down on one side of the stage. He drifts off to sleep and is soon snoring. After a few snores, he is again quiet.)

(MOUSE enters the stage from the opposite side and scurries around searching everywhere for food.)

MOUSE: (very excitedly) I must hurry. There's so much to do and so little time. I must gather food for my family. I've searched everywhere and still haven't found so much as a single acorn! There has to be something around here that I can eat. I'll just keep looking. (MOUSE's scurrying has brought him next to LION. MOUSE looks closely at LION's sleeping body.) What in the world is this? I just know it's something good to eat! I'll take a little bite and find out.

(MOUSE "bites" into LION. LION wakes up with a tremendous roar, sending MOUSE scurrying to safety on the other side of the stage.)

LION: (looking around) Who dares to bite the King of Beasts? (sees MOUSE) So it's you, is it? I'll soon teach you a lesson, you pesky, troublesome little mouse. Prepare to die!

MOUSE: Please don't eat me, King Lion, sir. I didn't know it was your royal body I was biting into. I thought it was something good to eat. Please spare my life. If you let me live, King Lion, sir, maybe someday I'll be able to do a favor for you.

LION: *You* do *me* a favor? How could a pesky little mouse like you ever be able to do me a favor? (LION begins to laugh.) Why, it's just impossible! *You* do *me* a favor!

MOUSE: (angrily) I may be small, King Lion, but I can still be of help!

LION: (impressed) Not many animals have the courage to stand up to me like you've just done. I admire your spunk, Mouse. As a reward, I will spare your life—you will be allowed to live. You may go now.

MOUSE: Yes, King Lion, sir. Thank you very much. (MOUSE scurries away and exits the stage.)

LION: (pleased with himself) How very gracious of me to allow that mouse to live. I think I'll take a walk around my kingdom.

(LION strolls along the stage and exits. From offstage there comes a horrible roar. Slowly, from offstage, LION's head emerges. The net has been thrown over LION's head and he is able to drag himself only as far as the corner of the stage.)

LION: (in desperation) Help! Help! I'm caught in this net. The hunters have set it as a trap for me. This is as far as I can drag myself. Please, somebody, help me! Maybe Elephant could untangle this net. Help, Elephant! Help! I can't stay trapped like this—the hunters are bound to be back soon!

(MOUSE appears at the opposite side of the stage.)

MOUSE: (looking around) That sounds like King Lion! (seeing LION) It is! He must be trapped! I'll go help him at once! (MOUSE scurries across the stage to LION.) King Lion, sir, I'm here to help you.

LION: How can you help me? You're just a tiny mouse. Maybe you could find Elephant or Rhinocerous and bring them here to help.

MOUSE: (looking around) I'm afraid we don't have time for that. The hunters will be back any minute. My teeth are very sharp, and I can chew through the ropes of the net. (MOUSE runs to different parts of the net, "chewing" the ropes.)

LION: Please hurry, the hunters will be here soon!

MOUSE: I'm chewing as fast as I can, sir. There's just one more rope over here. There! (MOUSE pulls the net off LION's body.)

LION: (shaking himself and roaring a triumphant roar) Free at last! It feels so wonderful to be free again! And I owe it all to you, Mouse. How can I ever repay you?

MOUSE: You don't need to repay me, sir. Remember, I told you that someday I'd be able to do you a favor. Now I have.

LION: I remember. And I also remember that I laughed in your face. I am truly sorry for not believing you, Mouse. I should have realized that size and strength are not always what is most important. The things that *are* important are cleverness and courage. And you, my friend Mouse, have plenty of both! Come my friend, let's leave here before the hunters return.

MOUSE: Coming, sir. (to the audience) Goodbye.

(LION and MOUSE exit the stage together.)

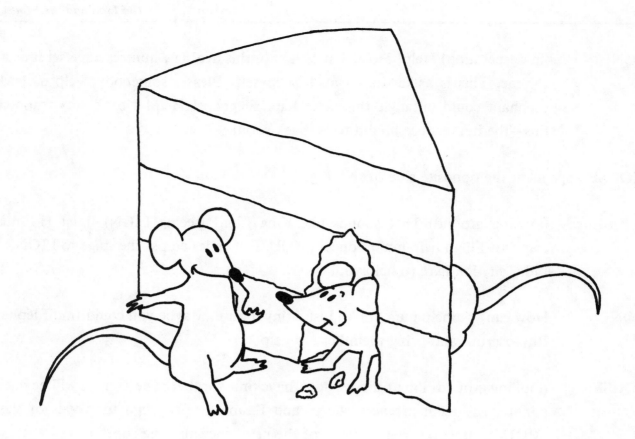

THE TOWN MOUSE AND THE COUNTRY MOUSE

CHARACTERS: Country Mouse (a humble animal who enjoys country life)
Town Mouse (his cousin, a sophisticated mouse about town)
Cat (intent on eating the two mice)
Dog (enjoys chasing Cat)

PROPS: A small leaf, a small piece of bread, an acorn (which Country Mouse carries onstage), a plastic piece of cheese and a plastic piece of cake (which Town Mouse carries onstage).

SCENE ONE: (COUNTRY MOUSE enters the stage, carrying "a small leaf." COUNTRY MOUSE sets this leaf down on the far side of the stage and then scurries offstage without noticing the audience. After a few seconds, COUNTRY MOUSE returns onstage carrying "a small piece of bread." COUNTRY MOUSE sets this bread next to the leaf onstage. Still oblivious to the audience, COUNTRY MOUSE scurries offstage. After a few more seconds, COUNTRY MOUSE returns onstage carrying "an acorn." COUNTRY MOUSE sets this acorn next to the bread and leaf, then finally notices the audience.)

COUNTRY MOUSE: (to the audience, slightly surprised to see them) Oh, hello. I've been so busy gathering food, I didn't notice all of you out there. I'm getting this food ready for my cousin's visit. I want everything to be as nice as possible because my cousin lives in town and doesn't have the chance to visit very often. (COUNTRY MOUSE looks at the food he has put on one side of the stage.) Let's see ... I have this leaf and this piece of bread and this yummy acorn. (to the audience) Doesn't this look like a delicious dinner?

(Before COUNTRY MOUSE gets a response from the audience, there is an offstage "knock" at the door.)

COUNTRY MOUSE: (to the audience) That's probably my cousin now. He's just in time to eat! (calling offstage toward the direction of TOWN MOUSE) Come in!

(TOWN MOUSE enters the stage from the side opposite COUNTRY MOUSE and his stash of food.)

COUNTRY MOUSE: (happily) Hello, Cousin. I'm so happy you're here! How was your trip?

TOWN MOUSE: (exhausted) Tiring! I haven't walked so far in years! You certainly live out in the boondocks!

COUNTRY MOUSE: I'm sure you're hungry after your walk here.

TOWN MOUSE: (agreeing) I certainly am! I'm so hungry, I could eat a whole wheel of swiss cheese!

COUNTRY MOUSE: (leading TOWN MOUSE to the opposite side of the stage to the food) Let's begin our dinner right now!

TOWN MOUSE: (shocked) What's this?

COUNTRY MOUSE: (proudly) This is our three-course dinner! Our salad is this leaf. Our main course is this piece of bread, and for dessert we have this delicious acorn!

TOWN MOUSE: (still shocked but trying to be polite) Cousin, you don't mean to tell me that you actually *eat* this kind of food!

COUNTRY MOUSE: Of course!

TOWN MOUSE: I guess I've gotten spoiled from living in town all these years, but Cousin, you deserve better food than this!

COUNTRY MOUSE: (not understanding) What kind of food do you eat in town?

TOWN MOUSE: (trying to impress his cousin) Cousin, you would not believe the variety of food! Why, there's any kind of cheese you could ever want! And there are cakes and cookies, pies and ice cream—everything to make a mouse fat and content! (has an idea) Cousin, why don't you come and live with me in town? You'll soon see that there's more to eat in the world than just leaves and acorns!

COUNTRY MOUSE: (undecided) I don't know whether I want to move. I like living in the country.

TOWN MOUSE: Just come back with me for a visit. You can stay as long as you like, and if you decide you don't like living in town, you can always come back here.

COUNTRY MOUSE: (making up his mind) I've always wanted to see what living in town would be like. Let me put this food away.

TOWN MOUSE: I'll help you.

(COUNTRY MOUSE and TOWN MOUSE both carry offstage the leaf, bread, and acorn. After a few seconds, they return onstage.)

TOWN MOUSE: Now, are you ready? You don't need to bring a thing, I can loan you everything you'll need!

COUNTRY MOUSE: (excitedly) This is going to be such fun! We'd better leave, we have a long walk ahead of us.

TOWN MOUSE: (tired just thinking about it) Don't remind me. But at least this time, I'm going back to civilization!

(COUNTRY MOUSE and TOWN MOUSE exit the stage together.)

SCENE TWO: (CAT enters the stage and leisurely walks across the stage, looking for mice. CAT exits the stage. Offstage, DOG's loud barks can be heard. Soon CAT runs across the stage followed by DOG. CAT exits the stage quickly chased by DOG. After a few seconds, COUNTRY MOUSE excitedly runs onstage.)

COUNTRY MOUSE: (to the audience) I can't believe I'm really here! Everything is so BIG here in town and there's so much going on all the time. (calling offstage toward the direction of TOWN MOUSE) Cousin, are you coming?

(TOWN MOUSE slowly enters the stage.)

TOWN MOUSE: (exhausted from the walk) Whew! I didn't think we'd ever make it here! I'll feel much better after I eat some decent food!

COUNTRY MOUSE: Is there anything I can do to help?

TOWN MOUSE: No, you just relax. You're *my* guest now. I'll go sneak into the kitchen and bring back some food.

(TOWN MOUSE exits the stage and returns shortly carrying "a plastic piece of cheese." TOWN MOUSE sets this cheese onstage.)

TOWN MOUSE: (proudly) Now, that's what I call food! Let's eat!

(TOWN MOUSE and COUNTRY MOUSE nibble away at the cheese but after a few seconds, they have eaten their fill.)

COUNTRY MOUSE: (with a sigh) That was delicious but I don't think I can eat another bite! There's enough cheese left for several more meals, shouldn't we put it away for later?

TOWN MOUSE: (carelessly) No, there's plenty more cheese where that came from! I'll just throw it away!

(TOWN MOUSE carries the cheese to the far side of the stage and throws it offstage.)

TOWN MOUSE: Well, Cousin, *you* might be full but I'm ready for dessert! I'll just go raid the kitchen again.

(TOWN MOUSE exits the stage.)

COUNTRY MOUSE: (to the audience) This is certainly the way to live!

(TOWN MOUSE returns, carrying "a plastic piece of cake." TOWN MOUSE sets this cake onstage.)

TOWN MOUSE: Just wait until you sink your teeth into this delicious cake, Cousin!

(TOWN MOUSE begins to nibble away at the cake and is soon joined by COUNTRY MOUSE. After a few seconds, they have eaten their fill.)

COUNTRY MOUSE: (almost ready to burst) I can't eat another bite! But it was certainly delicious. Should we throw the rest of this cake away?

TOWN MOUSE: Sure. There's plenty more waiting for us in the kitchen.

(COUNTRY MOUSE carries the cake to the far side of the stage and throws it offstage. Onstage, TOWN MOUSE and COUNTRY MOUSE rest contentedly and sigh.)

CAT: (from offstage) Meow, meow.

COUNTRY MOUSE: (terrified) What was that?

TOWN MOUSE: (calmly) Just the cat.

COUNTRY MOUSE: (still terrified) What do you mean, "just the cat"? We'd better run away before it sees us.

TOWN MOUSE: Don't get so excited. I've gotten used to that old cat. I outwit her every single day! I'll tell you when we should run.

COUNTRY MOUSE: (amazed) You mean that you and a cat live in the same house?

TOWN MOUSE: Sure. It keeps life exciting!

CAT: (from offstage but louder this time) Meow, meow.

COUNTRY MOUSE: (nervously) Is it time to run yet?

TOWN MOUSE: Almost. (looking offstage toward the direction of CAT) Now, let's go!

(TOWN MOUSE and COUNTRY MOUSE hurriedly run offstage. As soon as they have exited, CAT enters the stage from the opposite side. CAT searches the stage for the mice but without any luck. CAT exits the stage. After CAT has exited, TOWN MOUSE peeks his head onstage.)

TOWN MOUSE: (to the audience) Is the cat gone? (waits for a response from the audience) Good! (TOWN MOUSE enters the stage and calls offstage toward the direction of COUNTRY MOUSE.) The cat's gone now, Cousin, it's safe to come out!

(COUNTRY MOUSE enters the stage, still very frightened.)

COUNTRY MOUSE: Does this happen very often?

TOWN MOUSE: Sure. All the time. Don't worry, you'll soon get used to it.

COUNTRY MOUSE: (uncertain) I don't know if I'd like living in town.

DOG: (from offstage) Woof, woof.

COUNTRY MOUSE: (terrified) What was that?

TOWN MOUSE: (calmly) Just the dog.

COUNTRY MOUSE: (still terrified) You mean to tell me that you live in the same house with a cat *and* a dog?

TOWN MOUSE: Sure. Why not? I know it seems strange to you but don't worry, you'll get used to it.

COUNTRY MOUSE: (determined) I'm not going to get used to it because I'm leaving! I'm going back to the country—back where I belong—right now! Thanks for your hospitality, but I'm just not meant to live in town.

TOWN MOUSE: I think you're making a big mistake. Think about all the wonderful food here in town.

COUNTRY MOUSE: I'd rather eat leaves and acorns in peace and quiet than cheese and cake surrounded by a cat and dog. Goodbye, Cousin, and thanks for teaching me an important lesson.

(COUNTRY MOUSE exits the stage.)

TOWN MOUSE: (to the audience) My poor cousin. He just doesn't know how to live!

(TOWN MOUSE exits the stage.)

SCENE THREE: (COUNTRY MOUSE enters the stage.)

COUNTRY MOUSE: (sighing) Oh, it's *so* good to be back in the country! Living in town may be all right for my cousin, but I prefer the country! (to the audience) Listen to that. Ah, peace and quiet! No cats meowing or dogs barking. This is the life for me! (looking about the stage) I'd better get to work gathering food for my dinner. Goodbye.

(COUNTRY MOUSE exits the stage.)

THE JOHNNY-CAKE

CHARACTERS: Old Woman (a feisty woman who starts the Johnny-cake on its way)
Johnny-cake (a prairie-style thin cornmeal bread, usually fried)
Old Man (a peddler who is weary of the traveling life)
Dog (an enthusiastic animal who is very hungry)
Fox (the clever animal who finally outsmarts the Johnny-cake)

NOTE: The Johnny-cake can easily be made as a stick puppet. To make it "roll," all the puppeteer needs to do is rock the puppet back and forth as it moves across the stage.

SCENE ONE: (OLD WOMAN enters the stage.)

OLD WOMAN: (yawning) I sure had a good night's sleep. Now it's morning and time for breakfast. Let's see, what should I make? I could make porridge ... no, I had that yesterday. I could make fried cornmeal mush ... no, I don't feel like eating mush today. I've got it! I'll make myself a Johnny-cake! That'll hit the spot! I'll need cornmeal, flour, salt, and buttermilk. I've got all those things on hand, so I'll just go and mix it up! (to the audience) Don't go away—I'll be right back!

(OLD WOMAN exits the stage. She is humming offstage and returns shortly onstage.)

OLD WOMAN: There! I mixed that Johnny-cake up and poured it on the griddle to fry. I better be careful not to burn it. (sniffing the air) It smells like it's just about done. I'd better go flip it over.

(OLD WOMAN exits the stage. She lets out a loud scream offstage and runs back onstage.)

OLD WOMAN: I can't believe my eyes! I flipped that Johnny-cake but it jumped off my flipper and started rolling. I still can't believe it! (looks offstage toward the direction of the JOHNNY-CAKE) Why, it's rolling this way!

(JOHNNY-CAKE rolls onto the stage.)

OLD WOMAN: Stop, Johnny-cake! I want you for my breakfast!

JOHNNY-CAKE: Oh, no! I'm the Johnny-cake and I can go faster than you!

OLD WOMAN: We'll see about that!

(JOHNNY-CAKE rolls across the stage and exits. OLD WOMAN tries to grab it but the JOHNNY-CAKE is too fast and she falls down. OLD WOMAN picks herself up and remains onstage.)

OLD WOMAN: Who wants an old Johnny-cake, anyway? From now on, I'm sticking to mush!

(OLD WOMAN exits the stage. After a few moments, JOHNNY-CAKE rolls across the stage and then exits.)

SCENE TWO: (OLD MAN enters the stage.)

OLD MAN: It's getting late, I better get up and goin' this mornin'. What an awful night's sleep I had! I hate sleepin' on this hard, cold ground. Believe me, kids, it's a hard life bein' a peddler. Don't any of you ever become peddlers! I've been on the road for three weeks now, goin' from town to town tryin' to sell my wares and I haven't sold one single thing! (looks around him) What's for breakfast? Oh, that's right. All I got left to eat is baked beans! I'm so tired of eatin' baked beans! (looks offstage, toward the direction of the JOHNNY-CAKE) What's that comin' this way? It sure looks like a Johnny-cake. A Johnny-cake for breakfast would sure taste good!

(JOHNNY-CAKE rolls onto the stage.)

OLD MAN: Stop, Johnny-cake! I want you for my breakfast!

JOHNNY-CAKE: Oh, no! I'm the Johnny-cake and I can go faster than you!

OLD MAN: We'll see about that!

(JOHNNY-CAKE rolls across the stage and exits. OLD MAN tries to grab it but the JOHNNY-CAKE is too fast and he falls down. OLD MAN picks himself up and remains onstage.)

OLD MAN: Guess I'm not as spry as I used to be. I better try and find that can of baked beans.

(OLD MAN exits the stage. After a few moments, JOHNNY-CAKE rolls across the stage and then exits.)

SCENE THREE: (DOG enters the stage.)

DOG: Woof! Woof! Where did that rabbit go? I almost had him and suddenly he was gone. Darn, and I was hoping I'd have rabbit for breakfast! (looks offstage, toward the direction of the JOHNNY-CAKE) What's that coming this way? It looks like a Johnny-cake. I like to eat Johnny-cakes!

(JOHNNY-CAKE rolls onto the stage.)

DOG: Stop, Johnny-cake! I want you for my breakfast!

JOHNNY-CAKE: Oh, no! I'm the Johnny-cake and I can go faster than you!

DOG: We'll see about that!

(JOHNNY-CAKE rolls across the stage and exits. DOG tries to grab it but the JOHNNY-CAKE is too fast and he falls down. DOG picks himself up and remains onstage.)

DOG: A rabbit would taste much better for breakfast anyway. Maybe I can still find that rabbit.

(DOG exits the stage. After a few moments, JOHNNY-CAKE rolls across the stage and then exits.)

SCENE FOUR: (FOX enters the stage.)

FOX: (angrily) I am so mad! I was just about to grab this plump, juicy rabbit for my breakfast and a dog came blundering along, scaring that rabbit away! I am so hungry! (looks offstage, toward the direction of the JOHNNY-CAKE) What do I see coming this way? Could it be a Johnny-cake? YYUUMMMM! I just love to eat Johnny-cakes! I've got a delicious plan how to get that Johnny-cake for my breakfast. He's too fast for me to catch, so instead I'll just let that Johnny-cake come to me! I'll pretend that I'm a deaf old fox and then he'll have to come close. And then, before you can say "breakfast," he'll be it!

(JOHNNY-CAKE rolls onto the stage. When FOX doesn't say anything, JOHNNY-CAKE finally stops rolling and talks to FOX.)

JOHNNY-CAKE: I'm the Johnny-cake and I can go faster than you!

FOX: (looking around him) Did somebody say something? I'm not as young as I used to be and I can't hear very well. Please come closer.

JOHNNY-CAKE: (coming closer to FOX) I said, I'm the Johnny-cake and I can go faster than you!

FOX: I'm sorry, I still can't hear a word you said. I'm such an old fox. Won't you please come a little closer?

JOHNNY-CAKE: (coming still closer to FOX) I said, I'm the Johnny-cake and I can go faster than you!

FOX: I'm sure you can but that doesn't matter now! (FOX grabs the JOHNNY-CAKE and "eats" him in one gulp.) YYUUUMMMMM! That was the best Johnny-cake I've ever eaten! (to the audience) After all, that's what Johnny-cakes are for! Next time you see a Johnny-cake rolling by, please let me know. Goodbye.

(FOX exits the stage.)

SODY SALERATUS

CHARACTERS: Old Woman (a no-nonsense woman who needs sody saleratus for her biscuits)
Boy and Girl (her children who are sent to fetch the sody saleratus)
Rabbit (the family's pet who saves the day)
Bear (a very hungry animal who eats the family but is fooled by the rabbit)

PROPS: A small paper or cloth sack with the words "sody saleratus" written on it.

NOTE: This traditional Appalachian story usually has a squirrel defeating the bear by jumping from branch to branch of a tree. The bear follows the squirrel and falls, splitting open to reveal the other characters. In translating this story into a puppet play, I changed the squirrel to a rabbit who defeats the bear by challenging him to a jumping contest. Also, if desired, the puppeteer can ask the audience to join in with the "sody saleratus" song each character sings.

SCENE ONE: (OLD WOMAN enters the stage.)

OLD WOMAN: (to the audience) Hello, everybody! Sure glad you could join us today. It's time for me to get some vittles on the table. I think I'll make some stew and biscuits. I've got everything I'll need for the stew but let's see if I've got everything for the biscuits. (thinking out loud) I've got flour ... salt, shortening, milk, sody saleratus ... darn, I'm all out of sody saleratus! Well, I can't make my biscuits without sody saleratus. I tried one time and my biscuits were as hard and as flat as rocks! Guess I'll have to send my boy to go and fetch some sody saleratus home from the store. (calling offstage toward the direction of BOY) Boy! Boy! Get in here!

(BOY enters the stage.)

OLD WOMAN: (to BOY) Boy, I want you to go into town, go to the store, and get me some sody saleratus.

BOY: (eagerly) Yes, ma'am.

OLD WOMAN: Now be mighty careful going through the woods. There's lots of bears living in those woods. And don't you be wasting your time playing on the way back from the store. I want you to come right on home!

BOY: (has heard this all before) Yes, ma'am.

(BOY exits the stage.)

OLD WOMAN: (to the audience) Guess I'll go clean up the cabin while he's gone.

(OLD WOMAN exits the stage.)

SCENE TWO: (BOY enters the stage.)

BOY: (to the audience) Gosh, Ma doesn't send me on errands very often. It's so nice having a chance to go into town all by myself. (trying to remember) What was it that I was supposed to get? (remembering) Oh, yes—sody saleratus! (As BOY walks along the stage, he sings: "So-dy, so-dy, sody saleratus. So-dy, so-dy, sody saleratus.")

(BOY exits the stage and returns shortly from the same side, carrying the "sack of sody saleratus.")

BOY: (singing) "So-dy, so-dy, sody saleratus."

(BEAR enters the stage and sees BOY.)

BEAR: (to BOY) I'm hungry and I'm going to eat you up, little boy. You and your sody saleratus!

(Before BOY can say a word, BEAR "eats" him up, and his sack of sody saleratus.)

BEAR: (smacking his lips) That was good! I sure wish there was more to eat!

(BEAR exits the stage.)

SCENE THREE: (OLD WOMAN enters the stage.)

OLD WOMAN: (to the audience) Where in tarnation is that boy? I wonder what could be taking him so long? Well, I guess I'd better send my girl after him. (calling offstage toward the direction of GIRL) Girl! Girl! Get in here!

(GIRL enters the stage.)

OLD WOMAN: (to GIRL) Girl, I want you to go into town, go to the store, and get me some sody saleratus. I sent your brother there a long time ago and he still isn't back. He's probably playing along the way somewhere.

GIRL: (eagerly) Yes, ma'am.

OLD WOMAN: Now be mighty careful going through the woods. There's lots of bears living in those woods. And don't you be wasting your time like your brother playing on the way back from the store. I want you to come right home with that sody saleratus *and* your brother!

GIRL: (agreeing) Yes, ma'am.

(GIRL exits the stage.)

OLD WOMAN: (to the audience) Guess I'd better start making my stew for supper.

(OLD WOMAN exits the stage.)

SCENE FOUR: (GIRL enters the stage.)

GIRL: (to the audience) Gosh, I just love being sent into town on an errand. Just wait till Ma gets ahold of my brother—he'll really be in trouble! (trying to remember) What was it that I was supposed to get? (remembering) Oh yes—sody saleratus! (As GIRL walks along the stage, she sings: "So-dy, so-dy, sody saleratus. So-dy, so-dy, sody saleratus.")

(GIRL exits the stage and returns shortly from the same side.)

GIRL: (perplexed) I went to the store in town and the storekeeper said that my brother had already been there, bought the sody saleratus, and left. I guess he must be playing somewhere on the way home. I'll probably come across him real soon. (begins singing) "So-dy, so-dy, sody saleratus."

(BEAR enters the stage and sees GIRL.)

BEAR: (to GIRL) I'm still hungry and I'm going to eat you up, little girl!

(Before GIRL can say a word, BEAR eats her up.)

BEAR: (smacking his lips) That was good! These little children sure aren't very filling. I'm still hungry!

(BEAR exits the stage.)

SCENE FIVE: (OLD WOMAN enters the stage.)

OLD WOMAN: (to the audience) What's happened to everybody? I haven't seen hide nor hair of either of those children of mine! I'm starting to get worried. I'd better go and see what happened to them. (As OLD WOMAN walks along the stage, she sings: "So-dy, so-dy, sody saleratus. So-dy, so-dy, sody saleratus.")

(OLD WOMAN exits the stage and returns shortly from the same side.)

OLD WOMAN: (perplexed) I went to the store in town and the storekeeper said that my boy
                  had been there, bought the sody saleratus, and left. Then my girl was there,
                  asking about what happened to my boy. (worried) I sure do hope a bear hasn't
                  eaten them up!

(BEAR enters the stage and sees OLD WOMAN.)

BEAR: (to OLD WOMAN) I'm still hungry and I'm going to eat you up, old woman.

(Before OLD WOMAN can say a word, BEAR eats her up.)

BEAR: (smacking his lips) That was good! But even after eating that little boy, that
                  little girl, and that old woman, I'm still hungry!

(BEAR exits the stage.)

SCENE SIX: (RABBIT enters the stage.)

RABBIT: What's happened to everybody? First, the boy left, then the girl, and now the
                  old woman. (to the audience) Do you kids know what happened to them?
                  (waits for a response from the audience) A bear ate them up? Oh, how awful! I
                  guess it's up to me now to save them! I think I've got an idea how I can trick
                  that greedy old bear! I'll just go for a walk in the woods. (As RABBIT walks
                  along the stage, he sings: "So-dy, so-dy, sody saleratus. So-dy, so-dy, sody
                  saleratus.")

(BEAR enters the stage and sees RABBIT.)

BEAR: (to RABBIT) I'm still hungry and I'm going to eat you up, rabbit.

(Before BEAR can eat RABBIT, RABBIT quickly jumps out of his way.)

BEAR: (angrily) Stand still, rabbit! I'm going to eat you up!

RABBIT: Oh no, you aren't, Bear! I can jump higher than you can, so I'll be able to
                  jump out of your reach!

BEAR: I'm a bear and I can do anything a pesky little rabbit can do!

RABBIT: (challenging him) All right, let's see how high you can jump, Bear.

BEAR: (trying to jump but hardly getting off the ground) I didn't get a good enough start that time. I'll try again. (trys to jump again but can barely get off the ground) One more try! (With a heavy grunt, BEAR jumps off the ground but falls down with a heavy thud.)

RABBIT: (to the audience) Golly, I think he's dead. (RABBIT walks over to BEAR and examines him.) Yes, he certainly is dead. If I know anything about bears, I bet he swallowed everybody whole, without even bothering to chew! Maybe I'll still be able to get everybody out!

(RABBIT shakes the empty BEAR puppet. OLD WOMAN pops "out" from BEAR's mouth. OLD WOMAN exits the stage. RABBIT shakes the empty BEAR puppet. GIRL pops out from BEAR's mouth. GIRL exits the stage. RABBIT shakes the empty BEAR puppet. BOY pops out from BEAR's mouth. BOY exits the stage. RABBIT shakes the empty BEAR puppet. The sack of sody saleratus pops out from BEAR's mouth. The sack of sody saleratus exits the stage.)

RABBIT: (exhausted) Whew! That looks like everybody! I'd better hurry home. I don't want to miss out on any of those delicious biscuits!

(RABBIT exits the stage, dragging the empty BEAR puppet.)

SCENE SEVEN: (OLD WOMAN enters the stage.)

OLD WOMAN: (to the audience) That sure was a good meal! I ate seven biscuits!

(OLD WOMAN exits the stage. After a few seconds, GIRL enters the stage.)

GIRL: (to the audience) I'm so full, I can hardly move! I ate twelve biscuits!

(GIRL exits the stage. After a few seconds, BOY enters the stage.)

BOY: (to the audience) I've never been so full in my life. I ate eighteen biscuits!

(BOY exits the stage. After a few seconds, RABBIT enters the stage.)

RABBIT: (to the audience) I feel just great! And you know what? I ate thirty-one biscuits! I wish there were more biscuits to eat. Goodbye, everybody. If you ever have any problems with bears, just let me know.

(RABBIT exits the stage.)

LITTLE RED RIDING HOOD

CHARACTERS: Little Red Riding Hood (a very practical little girl)
                      Wolf (a somewhat bumbling animal determined to get some kumquat jelly)
                      Grandmother (at the moment, very sick with a bad cold)

PROPS: A basket for Little Red Riding Hood to carry (may be cut from felt and sewn to the puppet's hand) and a human-sized scarf (which is tied around Wolf's head).

SCENE ONE: (LITTLE RED RIDING HOOD skips onstage.)

RED RIDING HOOD: (to the audience) Hi there! My name is Little Red Riding Hood but all my friends call me "Red" for short. You're probably all wondering what I have in this basket, aren't you? Well, in this basket I have three jars of kumquat jelly. I'm taking them to my grandmother who is very sick with a bad cold. My mother always says the best thing for a cold is kumquat jelly. I'd like to stay and talk some more, but I'd better hurry to my grandmother's house. I'm going to take a shortcut through the forest. My mother always says that I should never go into the forest because there are wolves living there. But I'm not afraid of any wolf! Talk to you all later. Bye.

(LITTLE RED RIDING HOOD exits the stage. A few seconds later, she reappears from the opposite side from which she exited.)

RED RIDING HOOD: (to the audience) Hi, again! Boy, it sure is dark in this forest.

(WOLF suddenly appears on the opposite side of the stage.)

WOLF: (to LITTLE RED RIDING HOOD) Hello, there. Who are you?

RED RIDING HOOD: (not scared a bit) My name is Little Red Riding Hood, but all my friends call me "Red" for short. Who are you?

WOLF: I'm a wolf. Say there, Red, what do you have in the basket?

RED RIDING HOOD: Three jars of kumquat jelly. I'm taking them to my grandmother who is very sick with a bad cold.

WOLF: (to the audience) *Kumquat jelly!* That's my favorite food in the whole world! I've got to get my hands on that jelly! (to LITTLE RED RIDING HOOD) Say, Red, could I have some of that jelly?

RED RIDING HOOD: (shaking her head) No, I don't think so. My mother told me to take this jelly to my grandmother. She didn't say anything about sharing this jelly with a wolf. I better be going now. My grandmother is expecting me, and I don't want to keep her waiting. Goodbye.

(LITTLE RED RIDING HOOD exits the stage, leaving WOLF alone onstage.)

WOLF: (to the audience) I've just got to get that jelly! (thinks very hard) I've got it! I have a great idea! I'll hurry over to the grandmother's house before Little Red Riding Hood gets there. Maybe she'll change her mind and give me some of that jelly!

(WOLF exits the stage.)

SCENE TWO: (GRANDMOTHER enters the stage.)

GRANDMOTHER: (sniffling) Oh, what a horrible cold I have! I sure wish I had some kumquat jelly. That would certainly help my ... AA-AA-AA-CH-OOOOO! ... (GRANDMOTHER lets out a loud sneeze) ... cold!

(Offstage, there is a "knock" at the door.)

GRANDMOTHER: (to the audience) I hope that's my granddaughter, Little Red Riding Hood, but I'd better ask just to be sure. (calling offstage toward the direction of WOLF) Who's there?

WOLF: (from offstage, trying to disguise his voice but not doing a very good job) It's me, Grandma. Little Red Riding Hood. May I come in?

GRANDMOTHER: (happily) Oh, come in, dear, come in.

(WOLF enters the stage.)

GRANDMOTHER: (startled) You're not my granddaughter! You're a wolf! What are you doing here?

WOLF: I'm here for the kumquat jelly. I knew you'd never open your door to a wolf, so I lied and said I was Little Red Riding Hood.

GRANDMOTHER: Well, I don't have any kumquat jelly! I was just sitting here, wishing I had some. Maybe Little Red Riding Hood will bring some with her when she comes to visit me. But even if she does, I'm certainly not going to share it with a wolf! Now will you leave, or do I have to call a woodsman?

WOLF: (begging) Please let me have some of your kumquat jelly!

GRANDMOTHER: (very firm) *No!*

WOLF: (apologetically) Well, in that case, I'm going to have to do something I don't want to do. Sorry, Grandma.

(WOLF drags GRANDMOTHER offstage. WOLF returns alone onstage.)

WOLF: (to the audience) Don't worry. I didn't hurt Grandma. I would never do something like that! Why, I have a sweet little grandmother myself! I just locked Grandma in the closet so she wouldn't get in the way of that kumquat jelly. Little Red Riding Hood will be here any minute. I've got to think of some way to get that kumquat jelly! (thinking hard) I've got it! I'll pretend to be Grandma and when Red gets here, she'll never know the difference and then will give *me* all that wonderful kumquat jelly! Let's see, I'll need some kind of disguise. (looks around the stage and sees just the thing offstage) That's it! (to the audience) Don't go away. I'll be right back!

(WOLF exits the stage but returns a few moments later with the "scarf" tied around his head as his disguise.)

WOLF: (to the audience) I know it's not much but it's the best I could do on such short notice! I just hope it works!

(Offstage, there is a "knock" at the door.)

WOLF: (in what he thinks is a "grandmotherly" voice) Who's there?

RED RIDING HOOD: (from offstage) Grandma, it's me, Little Red Riding Hood! May I come in?

WOLF: Of course, my dear. Come right in.

(LITTLE RED RIDING HOOD enters the stage.)

RED RIDING HOOD: (to WOLF/GRANDMOTHER) I'm sorry that you're not feeling well. Mother sent you this kumquat jelly. That should help your cold! (takes a good look at WOLF/GRANDMOTHER) Gee, Grandma, you sure look horrible!

WOLF: (almost forgetting his grandmotherly voice) Oh, it's just because of this nasty old cold. I'll feel much better as soon as I have some of that kumquat jelly!

RED RIDING HOOD: (moving closer to WOLF/GRANDMOTHER) Gosh, Grandma, what a big nose you have!

WOLF: (still remembering his grandmotherly voice) Oh, it's just from blowing my nose! This cold is so nasty. AA-AA-AA-CH-OOOO! (WOLF lets out a very unrealistic sneeze.) I sure would like some of that kumquat jelly!

RED RIDING HOOD: (moving still closer to WOLF/GRANDMOTHER) Gosh, Grandma, what big, bloodshot eyes you have!

WOLF: (forgetting his grandmotherly voice entirely) Oh, it's just because of this horrible old cold. I'll feel so much better as soon as I eat some of that kumquat jelly. Please, give it to me!

RED RIDING HOOD: (finally discovering WOLF's true identity) Hey, you aren't my grandmother! You're that wolf I met in the forest! (LITTLE RED RIDING HOOD removes WOLF's disguise and lets the scarf fall behind the stage.) (to WOLF with anger) What did you do with my grandmother? If you hurt a single hair on her head, you're going to be sorry!

WOLF: (cowering with fear) I didn't hurt her, I promise! I just locked her away in the closet so she wouldn't be in my way. I *had* to get some of your kumquat jelly, and this was the only way I could think of. (begins to sob) You wouldn't share your jelly with me and neither would your grandmother. Please, don't hurt me! I didn't mean to trick you. I just wanted some kumquat jelly!

RED RIDING HOOD: (calmly) Golly, I didn't realize this kumquat jelly was so important to you. You can stop crying now, Wolf, I'm not going to hurt you. I'll make a deal with you. If you help me let Grandma out of the closet, I'll talk her into sharing some of this jelly with you.

WOLF: (amazed at her generosity) You would do that for me, after how I tried to fool you?

RED RIDING HOOD: Sure. You know, you're not such a bad wolf after all.

GRANDMOTHER: (a muffled voice from offstage) Let me out of here!

RED RIDING HOOD: (to the audience) That must be Grandma now. We'd better go let her out of that closet. Goodbye, everybody.

WOLF: (to the audience) Goodbye.

(LITTLE RED RIDING HOOD and WOLF exit the stage together.)

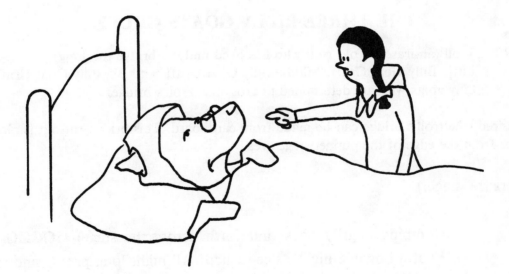

THE THREE BILLY GOATS GRUFF

CHARACTERS: Troll (an irascible old troll who has lived under a bridge too long)
Little Billy Goat Gruff, Middle Billy Goat Gruff, and Big Billy Goat Gruff (a family of billy goats who are determined to cross the Troll's bridge)

NOTE: If desired, the troll's bridge can be made from cardboard. This bridge cut-out is placed about six inches from the edge of the puppet stage area.

(TROLL enters the stage.)

TROLL: (stomping angrily back and forth across the stage) GGGGGgggggrrrrrrr! What a horrible night's sleep I had! All night long people and animals were crossing *my* bridge, going "trip-trap, trip-trap, trip-trap" right over my head! Why, it's enough to drive a troll crazy! Nobody had better get in my way today or I'll gobble them up! All I want to do is sit here by *my* bridge and go to sleep.

(TROLL walks to the far right side of the stage and settles down to sleep. Soon he is snoring loudly. After a few snores, he is again quiet. LITTLE BILLY GOAT GRUFF enters from the opposite side of the stage but does not see TROLL.)

LITTLE BILLY GOAT GRUFF:	(prancing happily along) What a beautiful day. It's a good day to visit the meadow and eat some of that nice green grass. I'll just cross this bridge.

(LITTLE BILLY GOAT GRUFF prances across the stage toward TROLL, making a "trip-trap, trip-trap, trip-trap" sound which the audience can be invited to join in making before the play begins. When LITTLE BILLY GOAT GRUFF is close to him, TROLL suddenly wakes up with a start.)

TROLL:	(very angry) Who dares to wake *me* up? (sees LITTLE BILLY GOAT GRUFF) Oh, it's you, is it? Well, just to teach you a lesson, I'm going to gobble you up!
LITTLE BILLY GOAT GRUFF:	(frightened but never losing his wits) Oh, Mr. Troll, you don't want to eat me! I'm just a scrawny, stringy, little billy goat. Why, I wouldn't even make a decent meal for a big, strong troll like yourself!
TROLL:	(flattered) Yes, I do eat a lot. (looks closely at LITTLE BILLY GOAT GRUFF) You're right, you *are* pretty scrawny and stringy.
LITTLE BILLY GOAT GRUFF:	Now I have a brother who is following me across this bridge. He should be here any minute. He's much bigger than I am and would make a much better meal. I think you should wait for him.
TROLL:	(thinks a moment) Maybe you're right. Get out of here! I'm going to wait for your brother, the big billy goat.
LITTLE BILLY GOAT GRUFF:	Thank you, Mr. Troll. Goodbye.

(LITTLE BILLY GOAT GRUFF exits the stage very quickly, crossing in front of TROLL.)

TROLL:	(greedily) I can hardly wait for that big brother billy goat to come along. I wonder how I should eat him. Gobbling him up would be a waste. Maybe I'll fry him. (thinks a moment) No, I had fried billy goat last week. Maybe I'll barbecue him. OOOooooohhhh, that sounds good! (TROLL becomes sleepy and yawns.) I'll just relax and think about that big billy goat!

(Once again, TROLL walks to the far side of the stage and settles down to relax. Soon he is snoring loudly. After a few snores, he is again quiet. MIDDLE BILLY GOAT GRUFF enters from the opposite side of the stage but does not see TROLL.)

MIDDLE BILLY GOAT GRUFF: (strolling happily along) What a beautiful day. It's a good day to visit the meadow and eat some of that nice green grass. I'll just cross this bridge.

(MIDDLE BILLY GOAT GRUFF strolls across the stage toward TROLL, making a "trip-trap, trip-trap, trip-trap" sound which the audience can join in with. When MIDDLE BILLY GOAT GRUFF is close to him, TROLL suddenly wakes up with a start.)

TROLL: (very angry) Who dares to wake *me* up? (sees MIDDLE BILLY GOAT GRUFF) Oh, this must be the big billy goat! (to MIDDLE BILLY GOAT GRUFF) Just to teach you a lesson, I'm going to gobble you up!

MIDDLE BILLY GOAT GRUFF: (slightly afraid but still thinking quickly) Oh, Mr. Troll, you don't want to eat me. I'm just a skinny, bony, little billy goat. Why, I wouldn't even make a decent meal for a big, strong troll like yourself!

TROLL: You don't look that skinny to me.

MIDDLE BILLY GOAT GRUFF: Oh, but I am! All skin and bones. Now I have a brother who is following me across this bridge. He should be here any minute. He's much bigger than I am and would make a much better meal. I think you should wait for him.

TROLL: You billy goats sure have lots of brothers! (pauses to consider the situation) Maybe you're right. Get out of here! I'm going to wait for your brother, the *big* billy goat!

MIDDLE BILLY GOAT GRUFF: Thank you, Mr. Troll. Goodbye.

(MIDDLE BILLY GOAT GRUFF exits the stage very quickly, crossing in front of TROLL.)

TROLL: (very greedily) I can hardly wait for that *big* brother billy goat to come along. He sure is going to make a lot of billy goat barbecue! Maybe I should have a party. No, that's not a good idea. I don't want to share my barbecue with anybody! (TROLL becomes sleepy and yawns.) I'll just relax and think about that *big* billy goat!

(Once again, TROLL walks to the far side of the stage and settles down to relax. Soon he is snoring loudly. After a few snores, he is again quiet. BIG BILLY GOAT GRUFF enters from the opposite side of the stage but does not see TROLL.)

BIG BILLY GOAT GRUFF: (striding confidently along) What a beautiful day. It's a good day to visit the meadow and eat some of that nice green grass. My brothers should already be there. I'll just cross this bridge and join them.

(BIG BILLY GOAT GRUFF strides across the stage toward TROLL, making a "trip-trap, trip-trap, trip-trap" sound which the audience can join in with. When BIG BILLY GOAT GRUFF is close to him, TROLL suddenly wakes up with a start.)

TROLL: (very angry) Who dares to wake *me* up? (sees BIG BILLY GOAT GRUFF) Oh, this must be the *big* billy goat! (to the audience) His brother wasn't lying — he certainly is *big*! (to BIG BILLY GOAT GRUFF) Just to teach you a lesson, I'm going to eat you up! Prepare to become barbecue, goat!

BIG BILLY GOAT GRUFF: If you think that you're going to eat *me*, Mr. Troll, you've got a lesson to learn yourself!

(BIG BILLY GOAT GRUFF walks slowly backward, ready to charge TROLL.)

BIG BILLY GOAT GRUFF: Here goes!

TROLL: (to the audience) This has not been a good day!

(BIG BILLY GOAT GRUFF charges at TROLL and tosses him far away offstage. TROLL lets out a loud yell. When TROLL is offstage, this yell becomes fainter and fainter until finally it stops.)

BIG BILLY
GOAT GRUFF: (satisfied with a job well done) There! Now this bridge belongs to everybody! After all, that's the best way to handle trolls. (to the audience) Don't you agree? I'm going to join my brothers now in the meadow. Goodbye.

(BIG BILLY GOAT GRUFF exits the stage.)

THE MONKEY AND THE CROCODILE

CHARACTERS: Monkey (a clever monkey who likes to eat)
Crocodile (not always as smart as he should be)

NOTE: This tale from India can be presented using a cardboard cut-out of Monkey's tree. This "tree" is placed on the far side of the puppet stage area, and it is from this tree that Monkey makes both her first and final appearances.

(CROCODILE glides onstage.)

CROCODILE: (to the audience) Hello. I'm glad you're all here today because this is a very special day for me. Today, I am going to catch Monkey and eat her heart! (surprised when the audience responds less than enthusiastically about this) You mean to tell me you don't eat monkey heart? Well, you don't know what you're missing! It's delicious! (getting back to his story) Every day I have been swimming in this river, watching Monkey swing from tree to tree, and I've finally figured out a plan to catch her! I'm going to be very friendly to Monkey and offer to take her across the river on a little ride. *Then*, when I have her in the water, I shall drown her and gobble down her heart! (looks offstage toward the direction of MONKEY) Here she comes now! (very pleased with himself) Ooooh, this is going to be such fun!

(MONKEY enters the stage from the top of her tree on the opposite side of the stage.)

CROCODILE: (to MONKEY) Hello, Monkey. Isn't it a beautiful day?

MONKEY: (suspiciously) Why are you talking to me, Crocodile?

CROCODILE: (a little too sweetly) I want us to be friends. I thought that since it is such a beautiful day, I would go for a little trip across the river to that big island on the other side. You know that island, don't you? It's the one with all the enormous fruit trees filled with ripe, juicy fruit! Would you like to come along with me?

MONKEY: (still suspicious but weakening) But how can I go with you when I can't swim?

CROCODILE: Don't worry about that. You can ride on my back and I'll take you across the river.

MONKEY: Are you sure this isn't a trick?

CROCODILE: (pretending to be offended) Monkey, don't you trust me?

MONKEY: (allowing her stomach to rule her head) I trust you. Just promise me you won't let me get wet.

CROCODILE: I promise!

(CROCODILE eagerly glides across the stage to where MONKEY is.)

CROCODILE: (delighted that his plan is working) Just climb on my back and hang on tightly.

(MONKEY climbs down the tree and carefully settles herself on CROCODILE's back.)

CROCODILE: Off we go!

(CROCODILE and MONKEY slowly glide along toward the opposite side of the stage.)

MONKEY: (enjoying herself) This is a fine ride, Crocodile!

CROCODILE: I'm glad you think so, Monkey.

(CROCODILE slowly dips below the stage level as if getting MONKEY a tiny bit wet.)

MONKEY: Crocodile, I'm getting wet!

CROCODILE: (apologetically) I'm *so* sorry! It's just hard for me to steer with a passenger on my back.

(CROCODILE and MONKEY continue on their way but suddenly CROCODILE dives down beneath the stage as if diving under the water level. After a few seconds, CROCODILE and MONKEY emerge again.)

MONKEY: (sputtering from being under the water) What happened?

CROCODILE: (sweetly) I'm so sorry, Monkey. The current was just so strong, it must have pulled me under. I'll go slower. Just be certain you hang on tightly.

MONKEY: I will, but please remember I can't swim!

CROCODILE: I realize how uncomfortable you must be up there, but just keep thinking about that wonderfully sweet fruit waiting for us on the island!

MONKEY: (hungrily) Yes, the fruit!

(CROCODILE and MONKEY continue on their way, but then CROCODILE dives down once more beneath the stage as if diving under the water level. They remain under for what seems to be a long time, then emerge again. MONKEY is definitely the worse for wear!)

MONKEY: (spitting and sputtering from being under the water) Crocodile, what are you trying to do? Are you trying to drown me?

CROCODILE: (dropping his sweet way of talking and being his greedy self) That's right! I'm going to drown you and there's nothing you can do about it! Once you're dead, I'll eat your heart!

MONKEY: (thinking fast) You want to eat my heart? (in mock indignation) Well, if *that* was your plan, I certainly wish you would have told me before we left! I left my heart up in my tree.

CROCODILE: You did what?

MONKEY: (explaining it to him slowly) I left my heart in my tree! I always do that whenever I go on a journey.

CROCODILE: (angrily) That was a stupid thing to do!

MONKEY: (in mock defensiveness) It's not *my* fault! And I'm certainly not going to go all the way back there just to get it for you! We're so close to the island, you can just drop me off there!

CROCODILE: (defiantly) I will not! I'm going to take you back to your tree so you can get your heart and bring it to me!

MONKEY: (enjoying playing along with CROCODILE) I guess you win, Crocodile!

(With MONKEY still on his back, CROCODILE returns quickly to where they began. As soon as they return, MONKEY scurries off CROCODILE's back and up her tree.)

MONKEY: (to CROCODILE from the top of her tree) Crocodile, my heart is up here! If you want it, just come up *here* and get it! (MONKEY laughs uproariously)

CROCODILE: (furiously) I'll get you yet, Monkey. Just you wait and see!

MONKEY: I can tell you this, Crocodile. I'm never going for a ride with you again!

(CROCODILE angrily storms offstage.)

MONKEY: (to the audience) I was lucky to outwit Crocodile that time, but I'm going to be extra careful from now on! Goodbye, everybody. I'll just take my heart and go look for food someplace else!

(MONKEY exits the stage, still laughing.)

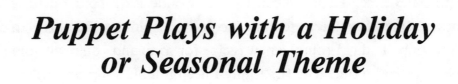

Puppet Plays with a Holiday or Seasonal Theme

WITCH'S WINTER KITCHEN

CHARACTERS: Witch (someone who loves to cook but doesn't always follow a recipe's directions)
Pig (Witch's friend who becomes her taste tester)

PROPS: A puppet-sized pot or cauldron, a tiny plastic toy animal (any type), a wrapped piece of hard candy, a small amount of plastic green grass, and a small plastic flower.

(WITCH happily enters the stage, humming to herself.)

WITCH: (to the audience) Hello, kids! Isn't it wonderfully cold outside? I just love cold weather! One of my favorite things to do on a cold day like this is to cook up a big pot of hot soup. Today I found a new recipe for soup and you're all going to help me make it! Won't that be fun? The first thing I need is a big soup pot, filled with water. (again to the audience) Now don't go away, I'll be right back!

(WITCH hurries offstage and returns shortly with the "pot or cauldron" which she then sets onstage. If an actual container is being used, WITCH places the subsequent props into the pot. If a cardboard cut-out is being used for the pot, then WITCH drops the subsequent props behind the cut-out and lets them fall in back of the stage, giving the illusion of placing them into the pot.)

WITCH: According to the recipe, the first thing I'm supposed to add is chicken. (looks about her) I don't happen to have any chicken but I know just the perfect thing!

(WITCH exits the stage and returns shortly with the "tiny plastic toy animal.")

WITCH: This little (WITCH names the type of animal) will be a good substitute for chicken. I'll just pop this into my soup pot. (WITCH places tiny plastic toy animal into the pot.) Okay, back to the recipe. The next thing I'm supposed to add is a pinch of sugar. (looks about her) I don't happen to have any sugar but I know just the perfect thing!

(WITCH exits the stage and returns shortly with the "wrapped piece of hard candy.")

WITCH: I picked this piece of candy up the last time I was at our local pizza restaurant. It'll be a good substitute for the pinch of sugar. (WITCH places wrapped piece of hard candy into the pot.) What do I need next? Let me see. Oh yes, I need to add two cups of spinach. Yecchhh! I don't like spinach so I'll just add something else. I know just the perfect thing.

(WITCH exits the stage and returns shortly with the "plastic green grass.")

WITCH: This was in my Easter basket. It'll be a good substitute for the spinach. (WITCH places plastic green grass into the pot.) Let's see, what next? Two cups of carrots. (looks about her) I don't happen to have any carrots but I know just the perfect thing.

(WITCH exits the stage and returns shortly with the "small plastic flower.")

WITCH: This little flower will be a good substitute for carrots. I'll just pop this into my soup pot. (WITCH places small plastic flower into the pot.) There! That seems to be everything! Now, the recipe says to simmer for three hours. Three hours! I don't want to wait that long for my delicious soup to be ready. I know what I'll do. I'll cast a magic spell on this soup. (to the audience) Will all of you help me? (waits for a response from the audience, preferably an affirmative one.) Good! Now, just repeat these magic words after me.
"Alla Ka-Zam"
"Alla Ka-Zook"
"Make This Soup"
"Cook!"
There, it's done. (WITCH sniffs loudly above the pot.) It even smells done. All I need now is someone to taste it for me. (looks about her and then looks offstage toward the direction of PIG) There's Pig! Pig, would you come here for a minute?

(PIG enters the stage.)

PIG: Hi, Witch! Hi, everybody!

WITCH: Pig, would you like to taste my soup? It's a brand-new recipe.

PIG: Sure. (PIG walks to pot and tastes the soup inside. Immediately PIG begins to cough.) Yecchhh! That tastes horrible! That's the worst-tasting soup I've ever had!

(PIG hurriedly exits the stage still sputtering and coughing.)

WITCH: Oh no! It can't be that bad! (WITCH tastes the soup.) Yecchhh! Pig was right, it *is* horrible! Well, I don't want to waste this entire pot of soup. (brightens up with an idea) I know! I'll cast another magic spell on it! (to the audience) Will all of you help me again with my magic? I'm afraid this soup is so bad that it will take all the magic we can manage! Now just repeat these magic words after me:
"Alla Ka-Zam"
"Alla Ka-Zissious"
"Make This Soup"
"Delicious"

I'm sure our spell worked that time. (WITCH sniffs loudly above the pot.) It does smell better. I'd better taste it first this time. (WITCH tastes the soup.) Why, it's wonderful. It's the best soup I've ever made! I'm sure Pig will agree with me. (calls offstage) Pig, would you come here for a minute?

(PIG peeks his head onstage.)

PIG: (cautiously) Witch, you aren't going to ask me to taste that horrible soup again, are you?

WITCH: Oh, it's much better this time! The kids and I put a magic spell on it. I think you'll like this soup now. Please taste it.

PIG: Okay. (very cautiously walks to the pot and tastes the soup) Hey, this soup tastes great! Gee, can I have some more?

WITCH: You can have as much as you'd like. Why don't you and I share this soup for lunch? (to the audience) Thanks to all of you for helping me with this soup. Isn't cooking fun? Now remember, don't try making this recipe at home unless you have lots of magic handy! Goodbye.

PIG: Goodbye, everybody.

(WITCH and PIG exit the stage, taking with them the pot.)

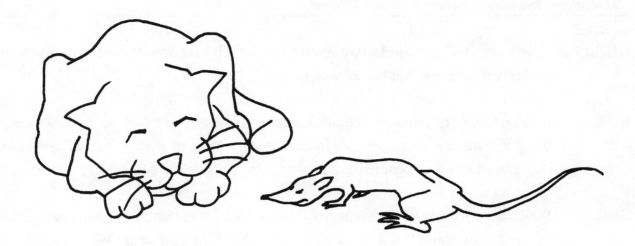

WHY CAT WAS LEFT BEHIND

CHARACTERS: Boy and Girl (two children who talk about the Chinese New Year and introduce the traditional tale)
Cat (a very proud feline)
Rat (a conniving creature who dislikes Cat)
Dog (a friendly animal who doesn't mean any harm to anyone)

NOTE: There are many variations of this tale in traditional Chinese and Buddhist folklore. For the purposes of this puppet play, I have used the character of an Emperor rather than Buddha and limited the number of animals that the audience sees to three. This play also serves as a springboard for discussing the Chinese New Year and the zodiac. At the end of this play, I have included a listing of the Chinese zodiac characters and their year rotation.

SCENE ONE: (BOY and GIRL enter the stage.)

GIRL: (to BOY) Gee, I can hardly wait to celebrate the New Year!

BOY: (confused) The New Year? What are you talking about? New Year's Day was weeks ago—remember January 1st?

GIRL: I wasn't talking about *that* New Year—I meant the Chinese New Year! Oh, it's such fun—days filled with special food, friends, and celebrating!

BOY: Gosh, I guess I don't know much about all that. But I *do* know that each year is named for a different animal. You know, like the Year of the Pig and the Year of the Dog—like that.

GIRL: That's right! There are twelve animals and each one has its own year. And then after twelve years, it starts all over again.

BOY: I know there are years named after some strange animals like Ox and Rooster, but one thing I've never understood is why there isn't a Year of the Cat? Cats have always been popular and lots of people have cats as pets, so why don't they have a Year of the Cat?

GIRL: Well, there are lots of different stories about why that happened. My favorite one has to do with how Rat played a trick on Cat. (GIRL has an idea) Why don't we have the animals show us how it all happened?

BOY: (excitedly) That's a great idea! I'd like to see that.

GIRL: (to the audience) So this is the story of why Cat was left behind....

(BOY and GIRL exit the stage together.)

SCENE TWO: (CAT leisurely enters the stage.)

CAT: (to the audience) Meow. It's such a difficult life being a house cat! All day long I have to make certain that Mouse or Rat don't get in the house. Those two little pests can do so much damage! They chew everything in sight. Now, don't get me wrong, even though it's hard being a Cat at times, I wouldn't want to be anything else! I certainly wouldn't want to be Dog—that slobbering ball of fur! (yawns) Maybe I'll go take a short nap.

(CAT settles down to sleep, curled up onstage. After CAT is sleeping, RAT scurries onstage. Seeing CAT, he is at first alarmed, but relaxes when he notices she is asleep.)

RAT: (to the audience) It's a good thing Cat is sleeping, otherwise I'd be a goner! (CAT stirs and RAT scurries further away from her.) Why should I be afraid of her? I have as much right here in the house as she does! (CAT wakes up.) Yipes! She's awake!

(RAT runs offstage, followed closely by CAT.)

SCENE THREE: (RAT enters the stage.)

RAT: (exhausted) That Cat chased me for nearly an hour! Whew! I'm tired. I just wish there was some way I could get even with her!

(DOG enters the stage.)

DOG: (excitedly to RAT) Hello, Rat! I've got the most wonderful news! The Emperor has invited all the animals to his palace. We're supposed to be there early tomorrow morning. It's very important because we're to be given a great honor!

RAT: A great honor, huh?

DOG: Oh yes, there's even a rumor that the Emperor may name a year after each of us! I'd like to stay and talk but I have to go tell Cat the news!

RAT: (has an idea) I know how busy you are, Dog. I'd be happy to help you and tell Cat all about the invitation.

DOG: (surprised) *You* want to tell Cat? I didn't think you liked her.

RAT: (slyly) Oh, that's all in the past. We have what you might call an understanding now.

DOG: (happily) Great! Just be sure to tell her it's *early* tomorrow morning. Goodbye.

(DOG exits the stage.)

RAT: (to the audience) I'll tell Cat … but then again, I might forget!

SCENE FOUR: (CAT enters the stage.)

CAT: (to the audience) It's been so quiet all morning. I haven't seen or even heard Mouse or Rat. Come to think of it, I haven't seen any animals at all. That's odd. Oh well, maybe they're all taking naps. What a nice idea. Maybe I'll take a little nap right now.

(CAT settles down to sleep, curled up onstage. After CAT is sleeping, DOG runs onstage, very excited.)

DOG: (to the audience) Where's Cat? (sees CAT) Cat! Wake up! Where were you? You missed your appointment with the Emperor!

CAT: (yawning) What appointment? What Emperor? What *are* you talking about, Dog?

DOG: Didn't Rat tell you?

CAT: (angrily) Rat didn't tell me anything! Would you please tell me what's going on here?

DOG: You see, the Emperor asked all the animals to come to his palace early this morning. Only twelve animals showed up. At first he was very angry that so few bothered to come, but then he said that he wanted to reward those of us who did come for our devotion to him. And so now each of us have a year named in our honor. Just think, every twelfth year will be the Year of the Dog! I'm sorry Rat didn't tell you. He promised me he would. That was very mean of him. (angrily) You just wait until I see Rat again! I'm going to give him a piece of my mind!

CAT: (through clenched teeth) That's nothing compared to what I'm going to give Rat when I see him again. Goodbye, Dog. Thank you for explaining everything to me.

(CAT exits the stage.)

DOG: Cat is so upset—I don't think she'll ever forgive Rat for this!

(Offstage, there is a loud shriek from RAT. Soon RAT scurries across the stage, right in front of DOG. RAT exits the stage.)

DOG: (to the audience) It looks like Cat has found RAT! I'd like to stay and talk but I'm going to run after Rat and tell him what I think about his trick!

(DOG runs offstage in pursuit of RAT.)

SCENE FIVE: (BOY and GIRL enter the stage.)

GIRL: (to the audience) So that was why Cat was left behind and not included with the other animals when the Emperor named the years. (to BOY) What did you think about the story?

BOY: Gosh, I felt sorry for Cat ... and for Rat, after Cat got ahold of him! I can't wait for the New Year—it's going to be fun! Why don't we start planning our celebration?

GIRL: That's a great idea. (to the audience) Goodbye, everybody and have a Happy Chinese New Year! Don't forget to find out in what year you were born!

BOY: (to GIRL) Golly, I hope I wasn't born in the Year of the Rat! (to the audience) Goodbye and Happy Chinese New Year!

(BOY and GIRL exit the stage together.)

The Animal Cycle of the Chinese Zodiac

RAT	OX	TIGER	RABBIT	DRAGON	SNAKE	HORSE
1900	1901	1902	1903	1904	1905	1906
1912	1913	1914	1915	1916	1917	1918
1924	1925	1926	1927	1928	1929	1930
1936	1937	1938	1939	1940	1941	1942
1948	1949	1950	1951	1952	1953	1954
1960	1961	1962	1963	1964	1965	1966
1972	1973	1974	1975	1976	1977	1978
1984	1985	1986	1987	1988	1989	1990

SHEEP	MONKEY	ROOSTER	DOG	PIG or BOAR
1907	1908	1909	1910	1911
1919	1920	1921	1922	1923
1931	1932	1933	1934	1935
1943	1944	1945	1946	1947
1955	1956	1957	1958	1959
1967	1968	1969	1970	1971
1979	1980	1981	1982	1983
1991	1992	1993	1994	1995

WITCH'S VALENTINE

CHARACTERS: Boy (an ordinary boy excited about Valentine's Day)
Witch (a kindly witch who learns about friendship)
Rabbit (an easily excited animal who loves to sing and make up songs)
Elephant (a slow-moving but kind-hearted creature who helps Witch)

SCENE ONE: (BOY enters the stage.)

BOY:　　　　(to the audience) I'm glad Valentine's Day is almost here. I've been busy making special valentines for all my friends at school and for my family. I've even made a valentine for my dog!

(WITCH enters the stage from the opposite side.)

BOY:　　　　(seeing WITCH) Oh no, it's a witch! Yipes! I'm staying out of her way!

(BOY quickly runs offstage.)

WITCH:　　　(shocked by BOY's behavior) Children today have such bad manners! I don't know what the world is coming to!

(WITCH exits the stage.)

SCENE TWO: (RABBIT enters the stage.)

RABBIT: (to the audience) Golly, I sure have a lot of work to do before Valentine's Day. The first thing I have to do is make up a special song. Let's see ... (RABBIT begins to sing, off-tune and rather badly.) "La, la, la. Valentine's Day is so much fun. La, la, la. I hope it's fun for everyone!"

(WITCH enters the stage from the opposite side.)

RABBIT: (seeing WITCH) Oh no, it's a witch! Yipes! I'm staying out of her way!

(RABBIT quickly runs offstage.)

WITCH: (becoming confused) I'm beginning to think there's something wrong with me. Could it be that I have bad breath?

(WITCH exits the stage.)

SCENE THREE: (ELEPHANT enters the stage.)

ELEPHANT: (to the audience) Oh boy, Valentine's Day is nearly here! I'm hoping someone sends me a valentine this year.

(WITCH enters the stage from the opposite side.)

ELEPHANT: (seeing WITCH) Oh no, it's a witch! Yipes! I'm staying out of her way!

(ELEPHANT runs offstage.)

WITCH: (very hurt) I can't figure out why everybody is so afraid of me. I'm really a very nice witch. Oh, I do wish everybody liked me! (brightens up) I've got an idea! I'll cast a magic spell on the whole world so that everybody will like me! (to the audience) My spell will be much more powerful if all of you help me. Will you? (WITCH waits for a response from the audience, preferably an affirmative one.) Good! Now just repeat these magic words after me:

"Alla Ka-Zam"

"Alla Ka-Zee"

"If This Spell Works"

"Everybody Will Like Me!"

I'm sure that spell worked. Now to try it out. (looks offstage toward the direction of BOY) There's that little boy walking right this way.

(BOY enters the stage but doesn't see WITCH.)

WITCH: Hello, little boy.

BOY: (seeing WITCH) Aaahh! A witch! Help!

(BOY runs offstage.)

WITCH: (confused) Maybe that magic spell doesn't work on people. I'll try an animal this time. (looks offstage toward the direction of RABBIT) I see Rabbit coming this way.

(RABBIT enters the stage but doesn't see WITCH.)

WITCH: Hello, Rabbit.

RABBIT: (seeing WITCH) Aaahh! A witch! Help!

(RABBIT runs offstage.)

WITCH: (unhappily) Now I know that magic spell didn't work at all! Nobody likes me and to make things worse, I can't even cast a spell! (WITCH begins to cry.)

(Hearing something, ELEPHANT peeks his head onstage.)

ELEPHANT: (to the audience) It sounds like someone is crying. (seeing WITCH) Oh, it's that witch. (ELEPHANT enters the stage and walks close to WITCH.) Why are you crying?

WITCH: (dejectedly) Nobody likes me. I tried to cast a spell on the whole world to make them like me, but it didn't work!

ELEPHANT: Witch, you can't make somebody like you. Friendships don't happen that way.

WITCH: Well, how do friendships work?

ELEPHANT: I don't exactly know, but I *do* know that friendships take time to grow. I don't have a lot of friends but I keep trying.

WITCH: Well, at least you didn't run away from me when you saw me this second time.

ELEPHANT: Of course not. You seemed unhappy, and I wanted to help you. Hey, I've got an idea of something that could help both of us. Would you like to make some valentines with me?

WITCH: (excitedly) Yes, that sounds like fun.

ELEPHANT: We can make valentines for all the people and animals who are afraid of you now. That way they'll know that you're a nice witch and not the nasty kind that we read about in stories.

WITCH: What a wonderful idea! You can come to my house. I'm sure I have some paper and glue and other things we can use. (to the audience) Maybe our magic spell worked a little after all! Goodbye, everybody. It looks like I'm going to have a happy Valentine's Day this year. I hope all of you do too!

ELEPHANT: Goodbye and Happy Valentine's Day!

(WITCH and ELEPHANT exit the stage together.)

THE LEPRECHAUN'S GOLD

CHARACTERS: Leprechaun (obsessed with keeping his gold safe)
Dog (simply concerned with finding a nice bone)

PROPS: A puppet-sized pot which we learn holds the Leprechaun's gold and, if desired, a small shovel (which can be cut from felt and sewn to Leprechaun's hand).

(LEPRECHAUN enters the stage.)

LEPRECHAUN: (to the audience) Hello, there. As you all know, St. Patrick's Day is almost here. I want to tell all of you a little secret … contrary to what most people think, it's not a good time to be a leprechaun. You see, many people believe that if they find a leprechaun and hold tight onto him, he'll tell where his gold is buried. Such foolishness! But people want to believe it, so around St. Patrick's Day, everybody suddenly goes mad trying to find a leprechaun and get his gold. So you see, I must find a safe hiding place for all my beautiful gold. (LEPRECHAUN looks around the stage. He stops at one spot and sighs with delight.) Aaaahhh! This looks like the perfect spot right here. (to the audience) Wait and I'll go get my gold.

(LEPRECHAUN exits the stage but shortly returns with the "pot" holding his gold. LEPRECHAUN sets this pot onstage.)

LEPRECHAUN: (to the audience) Isn't my gold beautiful? Oh, I just love gold! I even love the smell of it. (sniffs loudly over the pot of gold.) I'd better be getting about my work. I'll dig a hole for my gold right here!

(LEPRECHAUN quickly digs a hole, sinking further down below the stage, but soon emerging back onstage.)

LEPRECHAUN: (satisfied) There! That should do it! It's a nice, deep hole and no one will ever think of looking here. I'll just set my pot of gold down at the bottom and cover it up with dirt.

(LEPRECHAUN takes his pot of gold with him down the hole, leaves the pot, and returns onstage alone, pretending to stamp the dirt over the hole.)

LEPRECHAUN: Whew! What a relief! My gold is safe now. I'd better be off before someone sees me.

(LEPRECHAUN quickly scampers offstage. Offstage, barking can be heard and DOG runs onstage.)

DOG: (to the audience) Am I ever hungry! I'd just love to find a nice, juicy bone. (sniffs loudly around the stage, finally ending up at the spot where LEPRECHAUN has just buried his pot of gold) It looks like someone's buried something here. Probably a juicy bone. I'll dig it up and see.

(DOG begins to dig with his front paws, disappearing below the stage and emerging with the pot of gold which he then sets onstage.)

DOG: (perplexed) What is this? It's not a juicy bone, that's for sure! I wonder if it's something good to eat. I'll just take a bite. (DOG bites into the pot.) AAAAAOOOOOOWWWWW! I almost broke my mouth! Why would anybody bury something like this? Why, it doesn't even smell good. Yeeecchh! Guess I'll see if I can find something to eat.

(DOG exits the stage, leaving the pot of gold onstage. After a few moments, LEPRECHAUN returns onstage.)

LEPRECHAUN: (to the audience) I thought I heard some noise over this way. (sees his pot of gold onstage) What's my gold doing here? (perplexed) I thought I buried it. I was sure I buried it. Well, maybe in my hurry, I left it sitting here. I'll just quickly put it at the bottom of that hole I dug.

(LEPRECHAUN takes his pot of gold with him down the hole, leaves the pot, and returns onstage alone, pretending to stamp the dirt over the hole.)

LEPRECHAUN: Now, it's done. (looking about him) I'd better be off before someone sees me.

(LEPRECHAUN exits the stage. Once again, offstage barking can be heard and DOG bounds onstage.)

DOG: (to the audience) I still haven't had any luck finding something to eat. I'm *so* hungry! (sniffs loudly around the stage, finally ending up at the spot where LEPRECHAUN has buried his pot of gold) I smell something buried here. I'll just dig it up and see.

(DOG begins to dig with his front paws, disappearing below the stage and emerging with the pot of gold which he then sets onstage.)

DOG: (angrily) I think someone is playing a trick on me, burying this awful-tasting thing over and over! Well, I've spent enough time on this thing!

(DOG exits the stage in a huff, leaving the pot of gold onstage. After a few moments, LEPRE-CHAUN peeks his head onstage.)

LEPRECHAUN: (to the audience) I just wanted to be certain that my gold is still safe. (sees the pot of gold onstage and is horrified) What is *my* gold doing here? I positively know that I buried it last time! Some thief is trying to steal my gold. I'll teach that thief a lesson. I'll bury my gold one last time and then I'll wait for that thief and catch him red-handed!

(LEPRECHAUN takes his pot of gold with him down the hole, leaves the pot, and returns onstage alone, pretending to stamp the dirt over the hole.)

LEPRECHAUN: (to the audience) Now, I'll wait right over there for that thief to come back.

(LEPRECHAUN partially hides himself off to one side of the stage. Once again, offstage barking can be heard and DOG bounds onstage.)

DOG:
(to the audience) I can smell something. Maybe it's a juicy bone. (sniffs loudly around the stage, finally ending up at the spot where LEPRECHAUN has just buried his pot of gold) I can tell that something is buried here. I'll just dig it up and see what it is.

(DOG begins to dig but LEPRECHAUN suddenly pops out from his hiding place.)

LEPRECHAUN:
(accusingly) Stop it right there, Dog! Now, can you tell me why you were trying to dig up my gold? Were you going to steal it?

DOG:
(perplexed) Gold? Is that what this horrible-tasting stuff is? I was looking for a nice, juicy bone or something else good to eat. I can't understand why you would want to bury something like this.

LEPRECHAUN:
(figuring it out) So you didn't want to steal my gold?

DOG:
Gosh, no. All I want is a nice, juicy bone!

LEPRECHAUN:
(sweetly) Dog, my friend, I'll make a deal with you. If you promise not to tell another soul about where I've buried my gold, I'll buy you a nice, juicy steak. (DOG looks amazed at this.) That's right! A nice, juicy steak all for you!

DOG:
(eagerly) That sounds great. It's a deal!

LEPRECHAUN:
Well, let's be off. You can come with me and pick the steak out yourself. Just run on ahead of me, and I'll soon catch up with you.

(DOG exits the stage.)

LEPRECHAUN: Just one last thing ... (to the audience) Do all of you promise not to tell anyone about where I've buried my gold? (waits for a response from the audience, preferably a positive one) All right then, I can rest easy that my gold is safe and sound. Well, I'd better catch up with my friend Dog. Have a Happy St. Patrick's Day and goodbye now.

(LEPRECHAUN exits the stage.)

THE EASTER EGG HUNT

CHARACTERS: Pig (a likeable animal who believes in playing life by the rules)
Frog (the pompous official of this year's hunt)
Turkey and Wolf (two animals who are taking part in the hunt)
Fox (a selfish creature who is going to win the hunt no matter what)

PROPS: A puppet-sized basket filled with either plastic or wooden eggs. Ideally, this basket can be set on the shelf of the puppet stage. Otherwise, if a shelf is not available, a cardboard cut-out of a basket may be used.

SCENE ONE: (PIG enters the stage.)

PIG: Hi, everybody! I don't know whether you realize it, but today is a very special day! It's the day of the big Easter Egg Hunt! This is the fourth year I've been in the Egg Hunt but *this* year I'm going to win! The first-place prize this year is a six-foot-tall solid chocolate bunny rabbit! Yummm. I've been practicing for this Egg Hunt all year long. (looks offstage) I see the Egg Hunt is just about to start so I'll talk to you all later.

(FROG's voice can be heard coming from offstage.)

FROG: (offstage) Good day, fellow animals.

PIG: (to the audience) That's Frog. He's in charge of this year's Easter Egg Hunt!

FROG: (offstage) Welcome to the Sixth Annual Easter Egg Hunt. When I say "go," the Hunt will officially begin. On your mark, get set, *go*!

PIG: (to the audience) I'm off! Wish me luck.

(PIG hurries offstage.)

SCENE TWO: (After PIG exits, TURKEY scurries across the stage searching everywhere for eggs. TURKEY doesn't have any luck and so exits the stage. After a few seconds, WOLF bounces across the stage, also searching everywhere for eggs. Not finding any, WOLF also exits the stage. After WOLF has exited, PIG enters the stage.)

PIG: (to the audience as he searches the stage area for eggs) I'm having a very hard time finding eggs. I've looked everywhere and I've only found one egg! (suspiciously) There's something funny going on around here!

(PIG exits the stage.)

SCENE THREE: (FOX enters the stage with the prop basket filled with eggs. FOX sets the basket down on the stage.)

FOX: (to the audience) You see these eggs? They're all mine! I told myself that I was going to win this year's Easter Egg Hunt no matter what ... and I have! Do you want to know how I did it? (waits for a response from the audience) Okay, I'll tell you. Last night, Frog and the other judges were hiding the eggs for today's Egg Hunt. I was hiding too .. behind a tree, and I saw exactly where the judges hid all forty-nine eggs! Then the very first thing this morning, before the Egg Hunt had even started, I gathered up those eggs in my little basket here. Hee, hee, hee! Now for my first-place prize! I can hardly wait to bite into that six-foot-tall solid chocolate bunny rabbit!

(PIG enters the stage and sees FOX's basket filled with eggs.)

PIG: Gosh, Fox, where did you find all those eggs?

FOX: I'm not telling you, Pig.

PIG: (in awe of FOX's ability to find eggs) Gee, I could only find one egg!

FOX: (shocked) *You* found an egg? I was positive I found them all! Why, I even wrote down where the judges hid each egg so I wouldn't forget! You couldn't have found an egg!

PIG: (suspiciously) Did you say you wrote down where the judges hid each egg?

FOX: I didn't say that! You're making that up, Pig!

PIG: (still suspicious of FOX) I don't think you found those eggs honestly, Fox. I have a feeling you cheated.

FOX: I did not!

PIG: (hurt by FOX's cheating) Well, Fox, I'm sorry you had to resort to cheating. All I can say is that you certainly ruined this Egg Hunt for a lot of animals. Goodbye, Fox.

(PIG exits the stage.)

FOX: (to the audience) Who cares about other animals! I'll have that six-foot-tall solid chocolate bunny rabbit to keep *me* company! (looks offstage) Here comes Frog right now to award yours truly the first-place prize.

(FROG enters the stage.)

FROG: (clearing his throat) Fox, I'm here to present you with the first-place prize. Congratulations on finding all those eggs! We've never had any animal find so many eggs before. You've set a new record! Now for your prize.

FOX: (excitedly) I'm ready!

FROG:	This year we've had some complaints about our first-place prize. Many animals felt that a six-foot-tall solid chocolate bunny rabbit is just not a very healthy prize. Instead of all that chocolate, we have something just as exciting.
FOX:	(finding it all hard to believe) Just as exciting as a six-foot-tall solid chocolate bunny rabbit?
FROG:	Oh yes, this year's first-place prize is a year's supply of apples!
FOX:	(shocked) Apples?
FROG:	Yes, that's right, 365 apples! And they're all yours, Fox!
FOX:	(furious) Apples! I hate apples! I did all that planning and spying and work for a bunch of apples! Frog, you can keep your stupid apples *and* your stupid eggs! I would never have gone to all that trouble for apples!

(FOX storms off the stage, leaving behind the basket filled with eggs.)

| FROG: | (perplexed) Oh my. What do we do now? I suppose since our first-place winner doesn't want to accept his prize, we'll award it to the runner-up of the Egg Hunt. Pig was the only other animal to find an egg, so he's the new winner! (calls offstage) Pig, would you please come here? |

(PIG enters the stage.)

| FROG: | Pig, because Fox declined his first-place prize, you are the new winner of our Sixth Annual Easter Egg Hunt! Congratulations! The judges have decided on a new first-place prize—a year's supply of apples! The apples will be delivered to you tomorrow morning. Once again, congratulations, Pig. |

(FROG exits the stage.)

PIG: (ecstatic over his good luck) Apples! Oh boy! This is even a better prize than a six-foot-tall solid chocolate bunny rabbit! (to the audience) Don't you agree? (waits for a response from the audience, which in all probability will be negative) You mean you'd rather have a six-foot-tall solid chocolate bunny rabbit? (shaking his head) There's no accounting for taste, I guess. (noticing the basket filled with eggs) I don't think Fox wants this anymore, so I'll take it along with me. Have a Happy Easter, everybody. Goodbye.

(PIG exits the stage, taking along the basket filled with eggs.)

EASTER RABBIT'S BASKET

CHARACTERS: Easter Rabbit (a very exhausted rabbit)
                 Wolf (a bumbling animal who steals the last Easter basket)
                 Pig (a resourceful creature who helps solve everything)

PROPS: A puppet-sized Easter basket and pair of sunglasses (cut from dark paper).

SCENE ONE: (EASTER RABBIT enters the stage with the "Easter basket" which he sets onstage.)

EASTER RABBIT: (to the audience) Whew! Am I ever tired! (yawns) I've been so busy delivering Easter baskets that I haven't had a chance to sleep in days! (yawns again) Now, there's just one more Easter basket to deliver, then I'm going to sleep for weeks! (yawns once again) Maybe I should take a short snooze, just to get my energy back. Then I'll deliver this basket. (EASTER RABBIT yawns and then nods off to sleep.)

(WOLF enters the stage.)

WOLF: (to the audience) This has got to be one of my least favorite times of the whole year! Easter is really a dumb holiday! All those silly little lambs and chicks and rabbits—Yecch! (notices EASTER RABBIT and sees that he is asleep) Gosh, that looks like the Easter Rabbit ... and I think he's asleep. No wonder with all those silly Easter baskets to deliver! Look, that's an Easter basket right there! (looks closely at the basket) Gee, it's kind of cute—I sure wish I had an Easter basket like this. (has an idea) Well, since the Easter Rabbit's asleep, he'd never know if I took it! I think I will—right now!

(WOLF sneaks quietly offstage, carrying the Easter basket.)

EASTER RABBIT: (suddenly waking up) Easter baskets ... uh, yes. Where am I? Oh, that's right, I fell asleep. (to the audience) You won't believe this but I just had an awful dream! I dreamed that someone stole my last Easter basket! (laughing) Aren't dreams funny? (suddenly looks around the stage) Where is it? What happened to my basket? It was right here. It's gone! Oh no! This means there's going to be one really disappointed kid tomorrow! (to the audience) Hey, maybe you know who took my basket! Did you see who stole it? (waits for a response from the audience telling him that WOLF took it) Wolf took it? Gosh, how am I ever going to be able to get it back from Wolf? (depressed) I'm just too tired to think about it all! Maybe my friend Pig will be able to help me. I'll go see him right now!

(EASTER RABBIT exits the stage.)

SCENE TWO: (PIG enters the stage.)

PIG: (to the audience) I'm sure glad that Easter is almost here! It's such a great holiday! All those cute little lambs and chicks and rabbits!

(Offstage, there is a "knock" at the door.)

PIG: (to the audience) I wasn't expecting anyone. I wonder who that could be? (calling offstage toward the direction of EASTER RABBIT) Come on in!

(EASTER RABBIT enters the stage.)

PIG: Hi, Easter Rabbit! What a coincidence! I was just telling the kids how much I like Easter!

EASTER RABBIT: (woefully) Pig, I'm in *big* trouble! I had only one more basket to deliver, and I was so tired that I fell asleep. While I was sleeping, Wolf came along and stole that basket — the kids saw it and told me! I've got to get that basket back, Pig! Otherwise, some kid is going to be awfully disappointed! Can you help me?

PIG: (eagerly) This sounds like just the kind of case for me! Don't you worry about a thing, Easter Rabbit. I'll get that basket for you. You go back to your warren and get some sleep and leave everything to me!

EASTER RABBIT: (gratefully) Thanks a lot, Pig. I knew I could count on you to help. (yawns) I'll go get some shut-eye. Goodbye.

(EASTER RABBIT exits the stage.)

PIG: (to the audience) I just thought of a great plan to get that basket back! But first, I'll need a disguise. A pair of sunglasses will be perfect! I'll see you all soon!

(PIG hurries offstage. While PIG is offstage and before WOLF enters, the puppeteer has time to pin the dark paper "sunglasses" on PIG as his disguise.)

SCENE THREE: (WOLF is heard sighing from offstage as if he is very depressed. After a few seconds, WOLF enters the stage.)

WOLF: (to the audience) You know, I thought it would be so much fun having my very own Easter basket. Well, it's not! I keep thinking about some poor little kid waking up Easter morning without a basket. (sighs)

(Offstage, there is a "knock" at the door.)

WOLF: Gosh, I don't get many visitors. I wonder who would want to see me? (calling offstage toward the direction of PIG) Come in!

(PIG enters the stage with a commanding air, impersonating a famous talent scout and wearing the sunglasses as his disguise.)

PIG: (very glibly) Hello, Wolf. You don't know me but I'm a world-famous talent scout. I'm here because I've heard that you're a great singer. That's just the kind of talent I'm looking for!

WOLF: (surprised) Me? You really mean it? Gosh, no one has ever said that about me before!

PIG: I'd like to sign you to a million-dollar contract! Just think, you'll be on television and in movies! Why, you might even be in a commercial!

WOLF: But don't you want me to sing for you, first?

PIG: Sure, sure. Why don't you sing something appropriate for Easter?

WOLF: Okay, here goes! (sings any Easter-type song — possibly "Here Comes Peter Cottontail" — but very, very badly)

PIG: (mercifully interrupting WOLF after only a few lines) That's just great! You're a born singer! Before we sign that contract, I'll need to be paid.

WOLF: Gee, what do you charge?

PIG: I'm very reasonable. This week, I'm charging an Easter basket!

WOLF: (happily) I have one of those and I'll be happy to give it to you! As a matter of fact, I really don't want it! You see, the basket isn't really mine. I took it from the Easter Rabbit and I've felt awful ever since. Please, take it away.

PIG: (dropping his disguise and just being himself) Wolf, I have to be honest with you. I'm not a world-famous talent scout — I'm just Pig! Easter Rabbit asked me to try and get that Easter basket from you, so I tried to trick you into giving it to me. I had no idea that you didn't want it! Why did you take the basket in the first place?

WOLF: I guess just because it was there and Easter Rabbit was asleep. You see, I've never had an Easter basket before.

PIG: If you don't want that basket anymore, why don't you return it to Easter Rabbit? He's really worried about it.

WOLF: (shyly) I'd feel funny doing that. Can't you return it for me?

PIG: No, Wolf. I think you should return it yourself. Easter Rabbit won't be angry with you—he'll just be happy to have it back!

WOLF: (giving in) Okay, I'll do it. Thanks, Pig. I'll go get that basket right now. Goodbye.

(WOLF hurries offstage.)

PIG: (to the audience) Gee, Wolf isn't so bad after all!

(PIG exits the stage.)

SCENE FOUR: (EASTER RABBIT enters the stage.)

EASTER RABBIT: (yawns) Now, it's time for that nap! (nods off to sleep and is soon sleeping soundly)

(Offstage, there is a "knock" at the door.)

EASTER RABBIT: (waking up) What's that? Oh, it's just the door. (calling offstage toward the direction of WOLF) Come in!

                          (WOLF enters the stage, carrying the Easter basket which he sets onstage.)

EASTER RABBIT: (very surprised) Wolf! What are you doing here?

WOLF: (meekly) I came here to return your Easter basket and tell you how sorry I am that I stole it. I really didn't want the basket—it's just that I never had one before!

EASTER RABBIT: Thanks for returning the basket, Wolf. Now I can deliver it to the kid that it belongs to! You sure have made some little kid awfully happy!

WOLF: Gee, I'm glad. I felt rotten about keeping the basket.

EASTER RABBIT: You know, you're not such a bad wolf, after all! This job of being the Easter Rabbit is getting harder and harder every year. I sure could use some help. I don't suppose you'd be interested in helping me next year, would you?

WOLF: Me? Help you? You really mean it?

EASTER RABBIT: Of course I do! I could really use a wolf who is as strong and as clever as you
                        are to help me deliver all those hundreds and hundreds of baskets!

WOLF: (delighted) Gosh, I'd like to help you.

EASTER RABBIT: (pleased) That's great! I'll talk to you about all the details next week, okay?
                        (yawns) After I deliver this last basket, I'm going to sleep for a few days.

WOLF: Okay, I'll talk to you later. (to the audience) I think I'm beginning to like
                        Easter! Goodbye.

(WOLF excitedly exits the stage.)

EASTER RABBIT: (to the audience) I'm sure glad Wolf returned this basket. I'd better get going
                        and deliver it! Hope all of you have a Happy Easter! And whatever you do,
                        don't bother me next week! (yawns) I've just got to get some sleep!

(EASTER RABBIT exits the stage with the Easter basket.)

THE BACK-TO-SCHOOL BLUES

CHARACTERS: Boy (excited about returning to another school year)
Girl (reluctant even to think about school)
Witch (a kindly witch who helps Girl change her mind)
Monster (what Girl becomes)

SCENE ONE: (BOY and GIRL enter the stage. BOY is happily skipping along while GIRL lags behind.)

BOY: (to GIRL in a scolding manner) Hurry up or we'll be late for school. I certainly don't want to be late on the very first day!

GIRL: I don't care if we are late. I hate school!

BOY: Well, I don't. I like school and if you don't hurry up, I'm going without you. (sees that GIRL isn't moving) Okay then, see you later.

(BOY exits the stage.)

GIRL: (to the audience) I don't know why summer vacation had to end. It's just not fair that I have to stop having fun and go to school! Animals don't have to go to school, so why should people? Hey, that gives me a great idea! If I were an animal, I wouldn't have to go to school. And I know just the person to help me … Witch! I'll go visit her right now!

(GIRL excitedly runs offstage.)

SCENE TWO: (WITCH enters the stage, humming contentedly.)

WITCH: (to the audience) I'm so happy that school is starting again. That way, all the kids will be busy during the day and I can finally get some serious baking done. I have so many new recipes for yummy Halloween treats, and I can't wait to try them!

(Offstage, there is a "knock" at the door.)

WITCH: (annoyed) Just when I didn't want to be disturbed. (looks offstage in the direction of GIRL) Come in!

(GIRL enters the stage.)

WITCH: (surprised to see GIRL) What are you doing here? Aren't you supposed to be in school right now?

GIRL: I'm never going to school again! That's why I came to see you. I want you to cast a magic spell on me and change me into an animal. If I'm an animal, I won't have to go to school. Will you help me?

WITCH: Are you sure you want to be changed into an animal? You may not like it.

GIRL: I'm sure. Please change me into an animal.

WITCH: I think you're making a big mistake but I'll help you. Let's see, what kind of animal would you like to be?

How about a bat?   (GIRL shakes her head "no.")
... a dog?   (GIRL shakes her head "no.")
... a rat?   (GIRL shakes her head "no.")
... a mouse?   (GIRL shakes her head "no.")
(running out of ideas) Well, what about a monster then?

GIRL: (excitedly) A monster—that's perfect! Monsters never have to go to school, and everybody is afaid of them so they can do whatever they want! I'd like to be a monster!

WITCH: If you're sure that you want to be a monster, we can go ahead. Ready?

(GIRL nods her head "yes.")

WITCH: (to the audience) I think I may need some help with this spell. Would all of you like to help me? (waits for a response from the audience, preferably an affirmative one) Good! Now just repeat these magic words after me:
"Alla Ka-Zam"
"Alla Ka-Zonster"
"Turn This Girl"
"Into a Monster!"

(GIRL begins to shake and suddenly disappears beneath the stage. After a few seconds, MONSTER pops up onstage.)

MONSTER: (speaking in the GIRL's voice) Gosh, it really worked! I really am a monster! (to WITCH) Thanks a lot. I can't wait to see what it's like being a monster. Goodbye, Witch. I'll see you later.

(MONSTER/GIRL exits the stage.)

WITCH: (to the audience) I hope she comes to her senses soon. In the meantime, I think I'll start off by baking Rotten Pumpkin Cake. (looking around her) Where did I put that recipe? (again to the audience) I'll talk to you all later.

(WITCH exits the stage.)

SCENE THREE: (MONSTER/GIRL runs onstage.)

MONSTER: (growling) Grrr. This is *so* much fun! I don't know why I didn't ask Witch to change me into a monster sooner!

(BOY enters the stage from the opposite side from MONSTER/GIRL.)

BOY: (to the audience, not seeing MONSTER/GIRL) I can't find her anywhere! She never showed up at school and I'm beginning to get really worried! (sees MONSTER/GIRL and is afraid) Aarrgghh! A monster!

(BOY runs offstage.)

MONSTER: He didn't even wait until I explained what happened! Gosh, I hope my family doesn't worry too much about me. Oh well, there's still a lot of fun monster-type stuff I want to try.

(MONSTER/GIRL exits the stage. Offstage, MONSTER/GIRL continued to growl and make other horrible noises.)

SCENE FOUR: (MONSTER/GIRL slowly enters the stage.)

MONSTER: (unhappily and to the audience) I've been a monster for a whole day. It's not as much fun as I thought it would be! Monsters like to sleep in dirt, and they eat horrible things like beetles and ants! And after scaring a few people, there's really not much else for a monster to do! I never thought I'd say this, but I wish I were a person again. Maybe Witch will turn me back into a girl. I'll go ask her right now!

(MONSTER/GIRL hurries offstage.)

SCENE FIVE: (WITCH enters the stage.)

WITCH: (to the audience) Oh, I've had such fun trying out new recipes! My favorite one is for Spider Web Surprise. You'll all have to be sure to stop by my house on Halloween night and sample some.

(Offstage, there is a "knock" at the door.)

WITCH: (slightly annoyed) I don't know why I'm always being bothered in the middle of important cooking! (looks offstage in the direction of MONSTER/GIRL) Come in!

(MONSTER/GIRL enters the stage.)

WITCH: Could this be the girl that I turned into a monster?

MONSTER: It is and I was wondering if you'd please change me back into a girl. Will you?

WITCH: Don't you like being a monster?

MONSTER: No, it's probably okay for real monsters, but I miss my family and friends. I even miss going to school!

WITCH: That's what I was waiting to hear! Are you sure you're ready to be changed back?

MONSTER: (enthusiastically) *Yes!*

WITCH: Here goes. (to the audience) I think I may need your help again this time. Just repeat these magic words after me:

"Alla Ka-Zam"
"Alla Ka-Pearl"
"Turn This Monster"
"Back into a Girl!"

(MONSTER/GIRL begins to shake and suddenly disappears beneath the stage. After a few seconds, GIRL pops up onstage.)

GIRL: (excitedly) Gosh, I sure feel better now! Thanks so much for changing me back into a person. I can't wait to go to school tomorrow! See you later, Witch, and thanks again!

(GIRL exits the stage.)

WITCH: Now, back to my recipe. (to the audience) I certainly hope that none of you want to be changed into monsters! (wearily) I think I'm just about spelled out for one day! Goodbye, everybody.

(WITCH exits the stage.)

THE PUMPKIN THIEF

CHARACTERS: Old Man (a cantankerous old man who is very proud of his pumpkins)
Pumpkin Thief (although I use an elephant, it can be any animal)

PROPS: A small plastic pumpkin on a stick (this same pumpkin appears onstage all three times that Old Man goes into his pumpkin patch).

(OLD MAN enters the stage.)

OLD MAN: (to the audience) It's that time of year again. Time to go out into my pumpkin patch and find the biggest, best, and most beautiful pumpkin of them all! I've spent all summer watching and weeding and watering those little darlings, and now it's all going to pay off.

(The small "pumpkin" appears at the opposite side of the stage from OLD MAN. OLD MAN walks along slowly toward the pumpkin.)

OLD MAN: (to the audience) There it is! The most beautiful pumpkin in the entire patch. It's the perfect color, the perfect shape, and the perfect size. And it will make a perfect pumpkin pie! Now I'll just pick this pumpkin and take it home with me.

(OLD MAN picks the pumpkin up and walks back to the opposite side of the stage, carrying the pumpkin.)

OLD MAN: (to the audience) I'll leave it here on the back porch while I go in the kitchen and get everything ready for my pumpkin pie.

(OLD MAN exits the stage. While he is gone, PUMPKIN THIEF appears on the opposite side of the stage from the pumpkin. PUMPKIN THIEF hums a tango, sees the pumpkin, looks both ways to make certain the coast is clear, then quickly steals the pumpkin and exits the same side of the stage from which he appeared.)

(OLD MAN enters the stage from the same side he exited.)

OLD MAN: (to the audience) Everything's ready for that pumpkin pie, I just need to cut up that pumpkin. (OLD MAN looks about him.) Where is it? (OLD MAN looks everywhere onstage.) That pumpkin was right here a moment ago. (figuring it all out) I bet I know what happened to that pumpkin. Some low-down, no-account pumpkin thief has stolen it! (to the audience) Am I right about that, kids? (waits for a response from the audience) I thought so! I know what I'm going to do! I'm going to go back into that pumpkin patch and find another pumpkin!

(The small pumpkin appears once again at the opposite side of the stage from OLD MAN. OLD MAN walks along slowly toward the pumpkin.)

OLD MAN: (to the audience) There's a pumpkin. It's not as beautiful as the first one I picked but it will have to do. I'll just pick it and take it home with me.

(OLD MAN picks the pumpkin up and walks back to the opposite side of the stage, carrying the pumpkin.)

OLD MAN: (to the audience) Now I'm going to set right here and hold this pumpkin. I'll wait for that no-account pumpkin thief to come back and try to steal it. Then I'll grab him! He'll be sorry about stealing *my* pumpkins!

(OLD MAN begins to yawn and slowly drifts off to sleep. He is snoring loudly. While OLD MAN sleeps, PUMPKIN THIEF once again appears on the opposite side of the stage. PUMPKIN THIEF hums a tango, sees that OLD MAN is asleep, looks both ways to make certain the coast is clear, then quickly steals the pumpkin away from OLD MAN and exits the same side of the stage from which he appeared.)

OLD MAN: (suddenly waking up) Where am I? I must have drifted off to sleep. (looks around for the pumpkin) Where's my pumpkin? (to the audience) Do any of you know what happened to it? (waits for a response from the audience) I am *so* mad! I'm going to fix that pumpkin thief if it's the last thing I ever do! I'll go get another pumpkin.

(The small pumpkin appears once again at the opposite side of the stage from OLD MAN. OLD MAN walks quickly toward the pumpkin.)

OLD MAN: There's a pumpkin. (to the audience) It's not as beautiful as the first two but it will have to do. I'll just pick it and take it home with me.

(OLD MAN picks the pumpkin up and walks back to the opposite side of the stage, carrying the pumpkin.)

OLD MAN: (to the audience) Now I'm going to set right here and hold this pumpkin. And this time, I'm only going to pretend to fall asleep. That Pumpkin Thief thinks he's so clever. I'll show him this time! (OLD MAN begins to snore very loudly, and it is obvious he is pretending.)

(PUMPKIN THIEF appears on the opposite side of the stage from OLD MAN. PUMPKIN THIEF hums a tango, sees that OLD MAN is asleep, looks both ways to make certain the coast is clear, then tries to steal the pumpkin. This time, PUMPKIN THIEF is grabbed by OLD MAN. In the struggle, the pumpkin is dropped and falls behind the stage.)

OLD MAN: (to PUMPKIN THIEF) Now I've got you! Let's take a good look at you. What were you doing stealing my pumpkins?

PUMPKIN THIEF: (frightened) Gee, I'm sorry I stole your pumpkins but I just had to! You see, you were going to make all those beautiful pumpkins into pie, and I couldn't let you do that! Halloween isn't too far away, and the kids are going to need pumpkins for jack-o'-lanterns. That's why I stole them.

OLD MAN: (amazed) Why, I plum forgot about Halloween and jack-o'-lanterns this year! It's been a long time since I've had kids around my house. (to PUMPKIN THIEF) Thanks for reminding me. I've got an idea. How about you and me going into my pumpkin patch and picking out some of the nicest-looking ones for the kids. Maybe we could even carve ourselves a jack-o'-lantern later.

PUMPKIN THIEF: That's a great idea! (to the audience) Goodbye, everybody, and have fun carving your jack-o'-lanterns for Halloween!

(OLD MAN and PUMPKIN THIEF exit the stage together.)

WITCH GETS READY

CHARACTERS: Witch (a kindly witch ready to fly off to a party)
Mouse, Cat, Monster (the creatures that Witch's broom changes into)

PROPS: A small broom.

(WITCH enters the stage.)

WITCH: (to the audience) Hi, kids! My favorite holiday is almost here. Do you know what that holiday could be? (waits for a response from the audience) That's right! Halloween! And today I'm invited to a pre-Halloween Party. I want to make sure that I look my very best! I've frizzed my hair. I've put lots and lots of make-up on my face. And my clothes are nicely wrinkled. All I need now is my transportation. I haven't seen my broom for quite a while. (looks around the stage) Where could that broom be? (calls offstage) Broom! Broom! Broom, where are you? Come here please.

(WITCH's "broom" suddenly pops up onstage.)

WITCH: (delighted) There you are. Now broom, I need you to take me to a party. Are you ready?

(The broom begins to shake and suddenly disappears beneath the stage.)

WITCH: (looking everywhere onstage) Where are you, broom? Where did you go?

(Suddenly MOUSE pops up onstage.)

MOUSE: Squeak, squeak.

WITCH: Oh no, my broom has turned into a mouse! (indignant) Well, I certainly can't go to that party riding a mouse, can I? (to the audience) Maybe if all of you help me, we can change this mouse back into my broom. Will you help me? (waits for a response from the audience, preferably an affirmative one) Good! Now just repeat these magic words after me:
"Alla Ka-Zam"
"Alla Ka-Zen"
"Turn This Mouse"
"Into a Broom Again!"

(The MOUSE begins to shake and suddenly disappears beneath the stage. After a few seconds, CAT pops up onstage.)

CAT: Meow, meow.

WITCH: Oh no, my broom has turned into a cat! (indignant) Well, I certainly can't go to that party riding a cat, can I? (to the audience) I hate to ask you this again, but will all of you help me once more? (waits for a response from the audience, preferably an affirmative one) Good! Now just repeat these magic words after me:
"Alla Ka-Zam"
"Alla Ka-Zen"
"Turn This Cat"
"Into a Broom Again!"

(The CAT begins to shake and suddenly disappears beneath the stage. After a few seconds, MONSTER pops up onstage.)

MONSTER: GGggrrrrr, GGggrrrr.

WITCH: Oh no, now my broom has turned into a monster! (indignant) Well, I certainly can't go to that party riding a monster, can I? I simply *have* to get my broom back! (to the audience) Will you please help me just one more time? (waits for a response from the audience, preferably still an affirmative one) Good! Now just repeat these magic words after me:
"Alla Ka-Zam"
"Alla Ka-Zen"
"Turn This Monster"
"Into a Broom Again!"

(The MONSTER begins to shake and suddenly disappears beneath the stage.)

WITCH: Well, at least that monster is gone! (looks around the stage) But I don't see my broom anywhere. Oh, I just don't know what to do!

(Behind WITCH's back, the broom suddenly pops up onstage.)

WITCH: (turning around) There you are! I'm so glad you've come back! Broom, we'd better hurry off to that party. We certainly don't want to be late. (to the audience) Thanks so much for helping me with my magic. Sorry to be running off so fast, but I don't want to miss a bit of that party. Happy Halloween to you all!

(WITCH and broom exit the stage together.)

THE HALLOWEEN COSTUME

CHARACTERS: Girl and Boy (two children busy planning their Halloween costumes)
Witch (a kindly witch worried about her lost bat)
Bat (Witch's pet who is enjoying his freedom)

PROPS: A puppet-sized straw hat which is placed on Girl's head and a square piece of fabric which is placed over Boy to resemble a ghost.

SCENE ONE: (GIRL and BOY enter the stage together.)

GIRL: Golly, I'm so excited about Halloween. It's not very far away. (to BOY) What are you going to be for Halloween?

BOY: I'm not telling, it's a secret.

GIRL: I'll tell you about my costume if you tell me about yours.

BOY: (shaking his head) Nope. I told you, it's a secret. No one is going to know until Halloween night.

GIRL: I don't know why you're making such a big deal about your costume. You'll probably just be a ghost like you were last year!

(GIRL exits the stage.)

BOY: (calling after her) You just wait, you're going to be really surprised when you see my costume!

(BOY exits the stage.)

SCENE TWO: (WITCH enters the stage.)

WITCH: (to the audience) Have any of you seen my pet bat, Boris? (waits for a response from the audience) Oh, I was afraid of that! I can't find him anywhere. I was taking Boris for a walk last night and he slipped out of his collar and flew away! I just have to find him. I hope nothing has happened to him. (calling offstage) Boris! Oh, Boris!

(WITCH exits the stage.)

SCENE THREE: (GIRL and BOY enter the stage together.)

GIRL: (to BOY) You're driving me crazy with this *big* secret about your Halloween costume! I'll make a deal with you. I'll show you my costume if you'll show me yours.

BOY: (uncertain about this) I don't know.

GIRL: (pleading) Please? I promise I won't tell anyone. Maybe I'll even be able to improve your costume.

BOY: Okay, but you can't tell *anyone*!

GIRL: (agreeing) I promise, I won't tell a soul! Now let's change into our costumes and meet back here.

BOY: Okay.

(BOY and GIRL exit the stage together. While they are offstage, BAT "flies" across the stage and exits. After a few seconds, GIRL enters the stage wearing the "straw hat" on her head.)

GIRL: I've got my costume on. (to the audience) I'm supposed to be a scarecrow. (calling offstage) You can come out whenever you're ready.

(BAT flies onstage from the opposite side and hovers.)

GIRL: (very impressed) Wow! That's a terrific costume! You look just like a bat!

(BAT makes a few chirping noises.)

GIRL: You even *sound* like a bat! You were right to keep your costume such a secret—it's great!

(BAT flies offstage.)

GIRL: (to the audience) Gosh, I'd better work on my costume a little bit more.

(GIRL exits the stage. After a few seconds, BOY enters the stage with the "square piece of fabric" draped over him.)

BOY: I've got my costume on. (to the audience) I may look like a ghost but I'm not. I'm an apparition! (calling offstage) You can come out when you're ready.

(BAT flies onstage from the opposite side and hovers.)

BOY: (very impressed) That is a fantastic costume! I can't believe it, you look exactly like a bat!

(BAT makes a few chirping noises.)

BOY: You even *sound* like a bat! Gosh, I sure need to work on my costume some more.

(BAT flies offstage.)

BOY: (to the audience) I still can't understand how she ever got the idea for such a great costume!

(BOY exits the stage. After a few seconds, both GIRL and BOY enter the stage from opposite sides. This time, they are without their costumes.)

GIRL: (to BOY) Gosh, you had a terrific costume!

BOY: Oh, mine wasn't so good. Your costume was the one that was terrific! How did you ever get the idea to dress up like a bat?

GIRL: (confused) Bat? I wasn't a bat. I was a scarecrow. *You* were the one dressed like a bat.

BOY: Bat? I wasn't a bat. I was a ghost—um, I mean an apparition.

(GIRL and BOY look at each other. There is a short pause.)

GIRL: (slowly) If you weren't a bat ... and I wasn't a bat ... then....

(Both GIRL and BOY let out a loud scream and run offstage.)

SCENE FOUR: (BAT flies across the stage and exits. After a few seconds, WITCH enters the stage.)

WITCH: (calling offstage) Oh, Boris! Boris, where are you? (BAT flies onstage.) Boris, there you are! Oh, I was so worried about you. Are you all right? (BAT replies with a few friendly chirps.) That's good! Now, let's go home, Boris. I have your favorite snack all ready … Grub Nuggets! (to the audience) I hope all of you have a very happy and safe Halloween and thank you for helping me find Boris. Goodbye.

(WITCH and BAT exit the stage together.)

TURKEY'S THANKSGIVING ADVENTURE

CHARACTERS: Old Man (a gruff old man preparing for his Thanksgiving dinner)
Turkey (the hapless creature being pursued by the Old Man)

PROPS: A piece of string, a small stick, and a net (which can be made by knotting together several pieces of string or cord).

(OLD MAN enters the stage.)

OLD MAN: (to the audience) Well, it's that time of year again. Thanksgiving is almost here. That's the day we give thanks for all the wonderful things we have. Things like a warm house and family and friends and, most important of all, *food*! After all, what *is* Thanksgiving without food? Every year I have a nice, plumb turkey for my Thanksgiving dinner. And every year I've gone to the store and bought that turkey. But this year it's going to be different! This year I am going to catch my own turkey, just like the pioneers used to do! I've got to think of just the right way to trap that turkey. (to the audience) Don't go away, I'll be right back.

(OLD MAN exits the stage, but returns shortly with a "piece of string.")

OLD MAN: (to the audience) With this rope, I'm going to trap that turkey around its legs. (looks around) This looks like as good a place as any to wait for a turkey. I'll settle down right here until one comes by.

(TURKEY enters the stage from the opposite side and walks along the stage as if pecking the ground.)

TURKEY: Gobble, gobble, gobble.

(TURKEY slowly moves closer to OLD MAN. When TURKEY is fairly close to him, OLD MAN tries to tie the piece of string around TURKEY's legs but is not quick enough. TURKEY escapes and runs offstage.)

OLD MAN: (angrily) Drat it all! I was sure that rope would work. Let me think of some other way to trap that turkey. (has an idea) I know! I've got just the thing!

(OLD MAN exits the stage, but returns shortly with a "small stick.")

OLD MAN: (to the audience) With this stick, I'm going to hit that turkey on the head. Then it'll be all mine. (looks around) This looks like as good a place as any to wait for that turkey. I'll settle down right here until it comes by.

(TURKEY enters the stage from the opposite side and walks along the stage as if pecking the ground.)

TURKEY: Gobble, gobble, gobble.

(TURKEY slowly moves closer to OLD MAN. When TURKEY is fairly close to him, OLD MAN tries to hit it on the head, but TURKEY escapes and runs offstage.)

OLD MAN: (livid with anger) Double drat it! I was just sure that stick would work. Let me think of some other way to trap that turkey. (has an idea) I know! I've got just the thing!

(OLD MAN exits the stage, but returns shortly with a "net.")

OLD MAN: (to the audience) This net is sure to work! I'll throw it over that turkey's head, and then it'll be all mine! (looks about him) This looks like as good a place as any to wait for that turkey. I'll settle down right here until it comes by.

(TURKEY enters the stage from the opposite side and walks along the stage as if pecking the ground.)

TURKEY: Gobble, gobble, gobble.

(TURKEY slowly moves closer to OLD MAN. When TURKEY is fairly close to him, OLD MAN throws the net over TURKEY, trapping it.)

TURKEY: (pitifully) Gobble, gobble, gobble.

OLD MAN: (to TURKEY) Gotcha! (to the audience) Now that I have this turkey, what do I do with it? I guess I'll have to kill it. But look at those big eyes and that cute little beak. There is no possible way that I can kill such a cute little turkey.

TURKEY: (agreeing with him) Gobble, gobble, gobble.

OLD MAN: I've got an idea! Turkey, how would you like to join me for Thanksgiving dinner?

TURKEY: (perplexed) Gobble, gobble, gobble?

OLD MAN: I'll make a bit pot of spaghetti and we'll have a salad and ice cream for dessert. How does that sound?

TURKEY: (accepting his invitation) Gobble, gobble, gobble!

OLD MAN: Then it's all settled! Here, let me take this net off you. (OLD MAN lifts the net off TURKEY.) (to the audience) Well, I hope all of you have a Happy Thanksgiving — whether you have turkey for dinner or whether you have spaghetti like us! Goodbye.

TURKEY: (saying goodbye) Gobble, gobble, gobble.

(OLD MAN and TURKEY exit the stage together.)

SANTA CURES A COLD

CHARACTERS: Elf (one of Santa's helpers who is named Rollo)
                 Santa (unfortunately, not feeling well at the moment)
                 Reindeer (everyone's favorite — Rudolph)
                 Mrs. Claus (Santa's wise and resourceful wife)

SCENE ONE: (ELF enters the stage.)

ELF: (to the audience) Hi, everybody! My name is Rollo and I'm one of Santa's elves. As you all know, this is a very busy time for all of us here at the North Pole.

(While Rollo is talking, there is a loud sneeze from offstage.)

ELF: (frightened) What was that noise? It sounded like thunder, or maybe it was an earthquake!

(Again, there is a loud sneeze from offstage.)

ELF: (perplexed) It can't be thunder because I didn't see any lightning. And it can't be an earthquake because I didn't feel the earth move. I've got to find out what's making that horrible noise. (looking offstage, toward the direction of SANTA) Here comes Santa. Maybe he'll know something about that noise.

(SANTA enters the stage.)

ELF: Hi, Santa. Did you hear those horrible noises?

SANTA: (sounding very congested) Yes, Rollo, I did. As a matter of fact, I'm the one who made those horrible noises! AA-AA-AA-CH-OOOO! (SANTA sneezes) I woke up this morning with an awful cold! My throat hurts and my head aches and I can't stop sneezing! Oh, Rollo, I feel just terrible! (very worried) What are we going to do, Rollo? Christmas is almost here and I have *so* much work to do! I just don't have time to be sick with a cold!

ELF: Don't worry, Santa. I'll think of a way to cure your cold. Just go and lie down and rest. I'll let you know as soon as I have a cure for your cold.

SANTA: (gratefully) Thanks, Rollo. I don't know what I'd do without you!

(SANTA exits the stage, sneezing.)

ELF: (to the audience) I simply must find a cure for Santa's cold! I'll try thinking really hard. (ELF strikes a "thinking" posture.) I've got it! I remember years ago when I was a little elf, my mother always said that the best cure for a cold was exercise! It always worked for us—maybe it will work for Santa! That's it! All Santa has to do is to exercise! (calling offstage, toward the direction of SANTA) Santa! Santa! I've thought of a cure for your cold!

(SANTA enters the stage.)

SANTA: (still very congested) Here I am, Rollo. What did you come up with?

ELF: (enthusiastically) I'm just sure it's going to work! It always worked for my family when I was a little elf! All you have to do is exercise!

SANTA: (confused) Exercise?

ELF: Sure. My mother always said the best cure for a cold was exercise!

SANTA: (determined) I'll try anything to get rid of this cold! What kind of exercise should I do, Rollo?

ELF: Why don't you start off with some jumping jacks?

SANTA: (trying to be a good sport) Here goes!

(SANTA tries to jump off the ground but can't. Instead, he collapses in a fit of coughing.)

SANTA: (weakly) I don't think exercise is going to work, Rollo.

ELF: (perplexed) Gee, maybe it only works for elves! Don't worry, Santa. I'll come up with another cure if it's the last thing I ever do! Just go and lie down and rest. I'll let you know if I think of something.

(SANTA gratefully exits the stage.)

ELF: (to the audience) I simply *must* find a cure for Santa's cold. I'm all out of ideas but maybe my friend Rudolph will have some. I'll go visit Rudolph right now!

(ELF excitedly exits the stage.)

SCENE TWO: (REINDEER enters the stage.)

REINDEER: (singing) "Deck the halls with boughs of holly. Fa, la, la, la, la. La, la, la, la. 'Tis the season to be jolly...."

(Offstage, there is a "knock" at the door.)

REINDEER: (to the audience) I wonder who that could be? (calling offstage toward the direction of ELF) Come in!

(ELF enters the stage.)

REINDEER: (cheerfully) Hi, Rollo!

ELF: Rudolph, I need your help. Santa has a horrible cold and we've got to cure him. Do you know of anything that will work?

REINDEER: (thinking hard) Well, when I was a little reindeer, my mother always said that the best cure for a cold was to sing!

ELF: (surprised) Sing?

REINDEER: Yes, it always worked for us! Just make sure that Santa sings as loud as he possibly can. That way, it's bound to work!

ELF: (gratefully) Thanks a lot, Rudolph. You've been a big help!

REINDEER: Anytime, Rollo. See you later.

ELF: Bye, Rudolph.

(ELF exits the stage.)

REINDEER: (to the audience) I sure hope Santa gets over his cold. We have a lot of work to do before Christmas!

(REINDEER exits the stage, singing.)

SCENE THREE: (ELF runs onstage, very excited.)

ELF: (to the audience) Rudolph was a lot of help! I just *know* singing will cure Santa's cold! (calling offstage, toward the direction of SANTA) Santa! I've got a cure for your cold that's sure to work!

(SANTA enters the stage.)

SANTA: (still very congested) What's this cure, Rollo?

ELF: I asked Rudolph and he said that singing always worked for his family when he
                was a little reindeer! So, all you need to do is sing!

SANTA: Is there any certain song I should sing?

ELF: How about "Jingle Bells"? And Rudolph said to sing it really loud!

SANTA: (still trying to be a good sport) Here goes. (SANTA sings) "Jingle bells, jingle
                bells, jingle all the way. Oh, what fun it is to ride in a "—AA-AA-AA-CH-
                OOOO! (SANTA sneezes) Somehow, I don't think singing is going to work,
                Rollo.

ELF: (reassuringly) Maybe singing only works if you're a reindeer. Don't worry,
                Santa. I'll come up with a cure! Just go and lie down and rest.

(SANTA exits the stage.)

ELF: (in a panic to the audience) What am I going to do? Santa just has to get rid of
                his cold! (sniffs the air loudly) What's that smell? (sniffs again) I smell
                something delicious! I wonder what it is? (looking offstage, toward the
                direction of MRS. CLAUS) There's Mrs. Claus. Maybe she'll know.

(MRS. CLAUS enters the stage.)

MRS. CLAUS: (pleasantly) Hello, Rollo.

ELF: Mrs. Claus, do you know what that wonderful smell is?

MRS. CLAUS: I certainly do, Rollo. It's the smell of my own special recipe for chicken soup.
                That's *my* cure for Santa's cold. All he needs is lots of sleep and plenty of my
                chicken soup. He'll be back to his old self in plenty of time for Christmas!

ELF: (surprised) Chicken soup! Gosh, are you ever smart, Mrs. Claus! I never would have thought of that! (to the audience) I guess everything is going to be all right after all. I hope all of you have a very Merry Christmas! Goodbye, everybody!

(ELF and MRS. CLAUS exit the stage together.)

SANTA'S REINDEER

CHARACTERS: Elf (one of Santa's helpers who is named Rollo)
                   Horse (one of the animals who have been pulling Santa's sleigh)
                   Santa (the North Pole's most important citizen)
                   Mouse, Dog, and Elephant (three of the applicants for the Horse's job)
                   Reindeer (the natural choice for the job)

PROPS: A puppet-sized scarf which Elephant wears.

SCENE ONE: (ELF enters the stage.)

ELF: (to the audience) Hi, kids! My name is Rollo and I'm one of Santa's elves. As all of you know, Santa's sleigh is pulled by reindeer. Well, I'm going to tell you a secret! A long, long time ago, Santa's sleigh was pulled by horses! That's right! Horses! How did the reindeer ever get the job? We're going to show you exactly how it all happened. Here we go!

(ELF exits the stage but returns shortly.)

ELF: (to the audience) Things have sure been busy around here.

(Offstage, there is a "knock" at the door.)

ELF: Golly, I wonder who that could be? (calling offstage, toward the direction of HORSE) Come on in!

(HORSE enters the stage.)

HORSE: (shivering) Excuse me, Rollo. I've got to talk to you about something very important. The other horses sent me to tell you that we're quitting. We've loved our job of pulling Santa's sleigh but it is just too cold here at the North Pole. We've all decided to move someplace where it's nice and warm—like Florida! Sorry to give you such short notice, Rollo but we just can't take this weather anymore! Goodbye, Rollo.

ELF: (to HORSE) Thanks for telling me and thanks for all your hard work. Have a safe trip to Florida. Goodbye.

(HORSE exits the stage.)

ELF: (in a panic to the audience) Oh no! Christmas is almost here! Without the horses to pull Santa's sleigh, how are we ever going to be able to deliver all the Christmas presents? Well, Santa is sure to think of something. He always does! I'll go see him right now!

(ELF exits the stage in a hurry.)

SCENE TWO: (SANTA enters the stage.)

SANTA: (to the audience) Ho, ho, ho! Even though it's such a busy time for all of us here at the North Pole, I still always get excited about Christmas!

(Offstage, there is a "knock" at the door.)

SANTA: (calling offstage, toward the direction of ELF) Come in!

(ELF enters the stage, still in a panic.)

ELF: (to SANTA) I know how busy you are, Santa. I just had to bother you!

SANTA: That's all right, Rollo. I'm never too busy for you. So how can I help you?

ELF: (reluctantly) Santa, I have really bad news. The horses have quit! They said they've enjoyed their job but it's just too cold up here at the North Pole for them and they're moving to Florida. Santa, what are we going to do?

SANTA: (reassuringly) Now, don't worry, Rollo. We'll think of something. Let's both think very hard.

ELF: All right.

(SANTA and ELF pace back and forth across the stage, deep in thought.)

ELF: (with an idea) I've got it! We can send all the presents through the mail!

SANTA: No, I don't think that will work, Rollo. The Post Office is busy enough this time of year!

(SANTA and ELF resume their pacing of the stage.)

ELF: (with another idea) I've got it! We'll deliver the presents by truck!

SANTA: No, Rollo, that would take far too long!

(Once again, SANTA and ELF resume their pacing of the stage.)

ELF: (with another idea) I've got it! Let's get some other animals to pull your sleigh! I'm sure there are lots and lots of animals who would like to be your helpers!

SANTA: That's an excellent idea, Rollo!

ELF: Thanks, Santa. And I know just the way to get those animals. We'll run an advertisement in the newspaper!

SANTA: Yes, that will be perfect, and I know exactly how it should read. Take this down, Rollo: "Wanted—energetic and dedicated helpers to pull Santa's sleigh. Apply in person at the North Pole."

ELF: Got it, Santa! I'll run to the newspaper office right away and have them print our ad in tomorrow's paper. See you later.

(ELF exits the stage.)

SANTA: (to the audience) Rollo is such a great help. I'd better go see how things are coming at the Toy Shop.

(SANTA exits the stage.)

SCENE THREE: (ELF enters the stage.)

ELF: (to the audience) That ad in the newspaper sure worked! It was just in this morning's paper, and already there are dozens and dozens of animals lined up outside, waiting to be interviewed. Just wait until Santa hears the good news! (looking offstage, toward the direction of SANTA) Here he comes now!

(SANTA enters the stage.)

SANTA: (to himself) Where did I put that list of Susie's? (sees ELF) Hello, Rollo. How's the ad going?

ELF: (enthusiastically) Just great, Santa! There are dozens and dozens of animals waiting outside. It looks like everybody wants to be Santa's helpers!

SANTA: (concerned) That's wonderful news, but I'm afraid I don't have time today to interview *all* of them myself. Would you help me, Rollo, by looking at their applications and choosing, let's say, three animals. Then send those three to me and I'll interview them.

ELF: (pleased) I'd love to, Santa! I'll have them ready in a jiffy and send them to you right away!

SANTA: Thanks, Rollo. I'll be waiting for them.

(SANTA exits the stage.)

ELF: Well, I'd better get started with those applications!

(ELF exits the stage.)

SCENE FOUR: (SANTA enters the stage.)

SANTA: (to the audience) I'll just settle down here and wait for Rollo to send in the first applicant.

(ELF enters the stage.)

ELF: (yawning) Are you ready for the first one, Santa?

SANTA: Whenever you are, Rollo.

ELF: Here goes!

(ELF exits the stage.)

SANTA: (to the audience) I don't know what I'd do without Rollo. He's such a big help to me!

(MOUSE enters the stage.)

SANTA: Ho, ho, ho! It's a mouse. Hello, Mouse!

MOUSE: (enthusiastically) Hi, Santa! I'm here to apply for the job of pulling your sleigh!

SANTA: (kindly) I'm sure that you're very strong, Mouse, but my sleigh gets very heavy. Are you sure you could pull it?

MOUSE: (adoringly) I know that I probably couldn't pull your heavy sleigh but I'd do anything for you, Santa!

SANTA: I have an idea. Mouse, would you like to work here at the North Pole? The elves need help painting the eyelashes on dolls, and we could certainly use a clever mouse like you!

MOUSE: (delighted) Oh, thank you, Santa! I'll start right now!

SANTA: That's wonderful, Mouse. I'm sorry you can't pull my sleigh, but you're going to be perfect for the elves' Toy Shop!

MOUSE: Goodbye, Santa, and thanks!

(MOUSE happily exits the stage.)

SANTA: (to the audience) I'm so glad that we could put Mouse to work! (calling offstage, toward the direction of ELF) Rollo, are you ready to send in the next applicant?

ELF: (from offstage) Here she is, Santa!

(DOG enters the stage.)

SANTA: Hello, Dog. Nice to see you here.

DOG: (sneezing) AA-AA-AA-CH-OOOO! Hello, Santa. I'm sorry but I can't seem to stop sneezing … AA-AA-AA-CH-OOOO! (DOG sneezes) It all started when I got here at the North Pole and got near your elves.

SANTA: (concerned) It sounds like you could be allergic to elves.

DOG: That could be it … AA-AA-AA-CH-OOOO! (DOG sneezes)

SANTA: Dog, I'm afraid we have lots of elves here at the North Pole. I'm sorry but I think it would be better for you if you went back home. Thanks for coming all the way up here. Goodbye.

DOG: Thanks, Santa. I think you're right. I'll be glad to get home and stop … AA-AA-AA-CH-OOOO! (DOG sneezes) … sneezing! Goodbye and thanks.

(DOG exits the stage.)

SANTA: (to the audience) It's too bad that Dog is allergic to elves. (calling offstage, toward the direction of ELF) Rollo, you can send in the next applicant.

ELF: (from offstage) Okay, Santa!

SANTA: (to the audience) I hope this one works out!

(ELEPHANT enters the stage with the "scarf" tied around his neck.)

SANTA: Hello, Elephant.

ELEPHANT: (shivering) Hello, Santa. Golly, it sure is cold up here at the North Pole! I never realized it would be like this!

SANTA: Yes, it is cold up here.

ELEPHANT: (still shivering) I don't think I would ever be able to live here. It's too cold!

SANTA: (concerned) I understand, Elephant. You go home where it's warm. Thanks for coming all this way.

ELEPHANT: Thank you. It was nice to meet you. Goodbye, Santa.

(ELEPHANT exits the stage, still shivering.)

SANTA: (unhappily to the audience) Oh my. That was the last one, and we still don't have a replacement for the horses.

(ELF enters the stage.)

ELF: (yawning) I'm sorry, Santa. I guess I didn't make very good choices.

SANTA: It's not your fault, Rollo. The job is just too difficult! Rollo, you've worked very hard and deserve a rest. Why don't you go take a nap, and we'll think of something after you're rested.

ELF: Okay, but as soon as I get some sleep, I'll be right back!

SANTA: Take your time, Rollo. Have a good nap.

(ELF exits the stage. While SANTA is onstage, there is an offstage "knock" at the door.)

SANTA: (to the audience) What could possibly happen next? (calling offstage, toward the direction of REINDEER) Come in.

(REINDEER enters the stage, holding the scarf that ELEPHANT had worn.)

REINDEER: (timidly) I'm sorry to bother you, Santa. I was walking by, and I saw this lying on the ground. Someone must have dropped it. Do you know who it belongs to?

SANTA: (dejectedly) It doesn't matter now—he won't be needing it anymore. Say, I haven't seen you around here before. Who are you?

REINDEER: I'm a reindeer and I live down the block in a big cave. There are a lot of us here at the North Pole. You've probably never seen us because we're kind of shy and quiet. But lately some of your elves have been very nice to us, bringing us cookies and snacks. And we've been helping them by lifting some of the heavier presents.

SANTA: (putting everything together) So, let me understand this. You live here at the North Pole? (REINDEER nods his head "yes.") You like the cold weather? (REINDEER nods his head "yes.") Are you allergic to elves? (REINDEER shakes his head "no.") Would you and your fellow reindeer like to help me by pulling my sleigh?

REINDEER: (very happily) Oh, yes! That would be a great honor!

SANTA: (relieved) This is just wonderful! Christmas will be according to schedule after all! And to think that you reindeer were right here at the North Pole all this time! Come with me, we have lots to talk about.

(SANTA and REINDEER exit the stage together. After a few seconds, ELF enters the stage.)

ELF: (to the audience) So you see, that's just the way it all happened! The reindeer were so perfect at pulling Santa's sleigh that they've been pulling it ever since! Have a Merry Christmas, everybody!

(ELF exits the stage.)

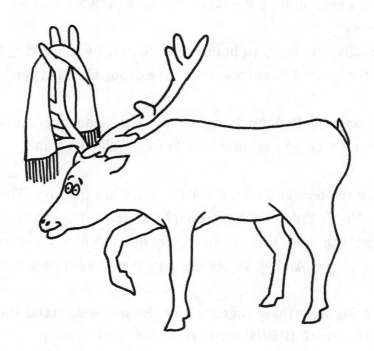

Puppet Plays with an Emphasis on Reading and Libraries

THE CASE OF THE DISAPPEARING BOOKS

CHARACTERS: Pig (a likeable animal who loves to read books on being a detective)
Librarian (can be either a man or a woman)
Monster (a creature who likes to eat books)

PROPS: Three small books (which are made by folding small sheets of paper—the covers may be decorated to resemble actual books) and a book with a bite taken out of it (actually a piece cut out of one corner).

SCENE ONE: (PIG enters the stage.)

PIG: (to the audience) Hi, everybody! You probably can't tell it by looking at me, but I'm a detective! Yes, really I am! I've been reading all about how to be a detective from books I've gotten from the library. I know everything there is to know about being a detective! All I need now is my first case!

(Offstage, there is a "knock" at the door.)

PIG: Sounds like there's someone at the door. (calling offstage, toward the direction of LIBRARIAN) Come on in!

(LIBRARIAN enters, carrying the "book" with the bite taken out of it.)

PIG: (to LIBRARIAN) Hi, there! (to the audience) It's the librarian. (to LIBRARIAN) If you're here about those overdue books of mine, I can explain.

LIBRARIAN: Oh, no. I'm not here about those. I'm here because the library needs your help. We've had something very mysterious going on lately at the library. Because you're always reading books on how to become a detective, I thought you might be able to help us.

PIG: Sure, I'm always happy to help the library. Why don't you start at the beginning. Tell me everything that happened.

LIBRARIAN: I first noticed it about a week ago. I came to work one morning and saw that the stack of books I'd left on my desk was gone. I thought maybe someone had moved them without telling me. I searched everywhere but still couldn't find them. They had simply disappeared! And every single day since then, the same thing happens. If books are left on tables or desks, they have disappeared by morning. But today I knew something was really wrong. I came into work this morning and found *this*! (LIBRARIAN shows the "book" with the bite taken out of it) You've got to help us find whoever it is doing this and make it stop! Otherwise, there soon won't be any books left in the library!

PIG:　　　　　　(astounded) I can't believe it! It looks like a bite has been taken out of this book. What sort of fiend would do something like this to a library book? Of course, I'll be glad to help you. Just leave everything to me. Can I check this book to check for clues? I'll be at the library tonight before closing. I'll catch whoever it is that is doing this awful thing.

LIBRARIAN:　　　Thanks, I knew we could count on you! I'll see you tonight.

(LIBRARIAN exits the stage.)

PIG:　　　　　　(to the audience) Oh, boy! My very first case! Let's see what clues this book might be able to give me. (PIG looks very closely at the book from all angles) HHHhhhmmmmmm. What's this? It looks like a piece of hair. But it's blue! Gee, this case may be even more dangerous than I thought!

(PIG exits the stage, carrying the "book.")

SCENE TWO: (LIBRARIAN enters the stage.)

LIBRARIAN:　　　(to the audience) It's nearly closing time and Pig still isn't here! I hope he remembers. (looking offstage, toward the direction of PIG) Here he comes now.

(PIG enters the stage.)

PIG:　　　　　　(to LIBRARIAN) I'm sorry I'm late. I've spent all day thinking of just the right way to handle this case. And I think I've got it! I'm going to get to the bottom of this mystery if it's the last thing I ever do! Now, just leave everything to me!

LIBRARIAN:　　　(hesitating) I don't feel right about leaving you here in a dark, deserted library.

PIG:　　　　　　I'll be fine. After all, I *am* a detective!

LIBRARIAN:　　　Good night, Pig. If you have any problems, give me a call!

(LIBRARIAN exits the stage.)

PIG: (to the audience) Now that I'm alone, I'll start setting my trap. Since books are what this thief is after, I've decided to set my trap with books! I'll go to the shelves and pull some of my favorites!

(PIG exits the stage and returns soon with one of the books.)

PIG: (to the audience) This is one of my favorites! (PIG can name an actual title and even tell the audience a little bit about it.) I'll set it right here. (PIG sets book onstage.) Now, I'll go get another of my favorite books.

(PIG exits the stage again and returns with another book.)

PIG: (to the audience) This is a really great book! (PIG can again name an actual title and tell a little bit about it.) This one will go right there. (PIG sets book onstage.) That's two books. I'll go get one more!

(PIG exits the stage again and returns with another book.)

PIG: (to the audience) I just *had* to pick this book! (PIG can again name an actual title and tell a little bit about it.) There! (PIG sets book onstage.) That should do it! (PIG yawns) Boy, all this excitement has made me tired! (PIG yawns again) Now, to sit back and wait for that thief! (PIG yawns once again.) I sure hope I can stay awake tonight! (PIG yawns once more and nods off to sleep. PIG snores loudly, then slowly quiets down and stops snoring.)

(While PIG is sleeping, MONSTER enters the stage. MONSTER looks around the stage, sees that PIG is asleep, and quickly grabs the book closest to him. MONSTER "eats" the book with delight and loud gurgling noises. PIG moves slightly and MONSTER hurriedly exits the stage.)

PIG: (waking up) What happened? I'm sure I heard something move! (to the audience) Did you see something? (PIG waits for a response from the audience) You did? A monster! Well, I'm going to wait right here! I'm sure that monster will be back! A criminal always returns to the scene of the crime! (PIG yawns) Gosh, I sure am tired! But I just can't fall asleep! Sherlock Holmes would never, ever fall asleep on a case! (PIG yawns again.) I've just *got* to stay awake! (PIG again falls asleep. PIG snores loudly, then slowly quiets down and stops snoring.)

(While PIG is sleeping, MONSTER enters the stage. MONSTER looks around the stage, sees that PIG is asleep, and quickly grabs the book closest to him. MONSTER eats the book with delight and loud gurgling noises. PIG moves slightly and MONSTER hurriedly exits the stage.)

PIG: (waking up) What happened? Oh, no, not again! (to the audience) Was that monster back again? (PIG waits for a response from the audience.) He was! Well, this time I'm staying awake no matter what! I'm staying right here and absolutely nothing is going to make me (PIG yawns) fall asleep. (PIG yawns again.) Maybe I'll rest my eyes for a minute! (PIG again falls asleep. PIG snores loudly, then slowly quiets down and stops snoring.)

(While PIG is sleeping, MONSTER again enters the stage. MONSTER looks around the stage, sees that PIG is asleep, and quickly grabs the book closest to him. MONSTER eats the book with delight and more loud gurgling noises. MONSTER lets out a very loud burp which wakes PIG. Before MONSTER can escape, PIG has a firm grip on him.)

PIG: Now listen here, Monster! Tell me what you're doing here in the library and what you've done to all their books!

MONSTER: (pleadingly) Oh please, don't hurt me! I didn't mean to do anything wrong! All I did was to eat the food they left here for me!

PIG: (confused) What food?

MONSTER: The yummy things they left for me on the tables and desks and tonight, on the floor! They are delicious! My favorites are the red ones!

PIG: (trying to figure it out) You mean to tell me, you actually *eat* books?

MONSTER: Is that what they are called? Books?

PIG: Yes, that's what they are called! And they aren't meant to be eaten! Books are supposed to be read!

MONSTER: (agreeing) Yes, that is a good idea! All books should be red. The red ones are delicious!

PIG: (angrily) That's not what I mean! You are supposed to *read* books, not eat them!

MONSTER: (confused) What is reading?

PIG: (amazed) You mean that you don't know how to read? (MONSTER shakes his head "no.") Why, reading is great! When I read a book, I can go anywhere I want!

MONSTER: It sounds like fun to read! How can I learn?

PIG: I'll make a deal with you, Monster. If you promise never to eat another book, I'll teach you to read. Now, do you promise?

MONSTER: (not certain) It will be very hard. Books are so tasty! (agrees) Okay! I promise never to eat another book!

PIG: (happily) Stick with me, Monster, and you'll find a better way to "eat" books! (to the audience) Thanks for helping me solve this case. Goodbye and have lots of fun reading books!

MONSTER: (to the audience) Goodbye!

(PIG and MONSTER exit the stage together.)

MONSTER READS

CHARACTERS: Monster (has recently learned how to read and can't get enough of it)
                   Pig, Lamb, and Fox (friends of Monster)
                   Librarian (can be either a man or woman)

NOTE: This play is intended as a follow-up to *The Case of the Disappearing Books* but can easily be enjoyed on its own.

SCENE ONE: (MONSTER enters the stage.)

MONSTER: (seeing the audience) Hi, everybody! I am so glad that I learned how to read. It is so much fun! I am on my way to the library right now to find a good book to read. (looks offstage toward the direction of PIG) Look, there's my friend Pig! Hello, Pig.

(PIG enters the stage.)

PIG: Hi, Monster. What are you up to today?

MONSTER: I am on my way to the library to find a good book to read. Do you have any ideas?

PIG: I sure do! One of my favorite books is *The Three Little Pigs*. It's a wonderful story about three smart little pigs who trick a mean old wolf. I think you'll like reading that book.

MONSTER: Thank you, Pig. That sounds like a good book … *The Three Little Pigs*.

PIG: Have fun at the library, Monster. I'll see you later.

(PIG exits the stage.)

MONSTER: (trying to concentrate) I have to remember the name of Pig's book. It is *The Three Little Pigs*. (looks offstage toward the direction of LAMB) Look, there's my friend Lamb! Hello, Lamb.

(LAMB shyly enters the stage.)

LAMB: Hello, Monster. Where are you off to today?

MONSTER: I am on my way to the library to find a good book to read. I just saw Pig and he told me about a wonderful book called *The Three Little Pigs*. I am going to ask for that book at the library.

LAMB: That's a good story, but I know another one you'll like. It's called *The Boy Who Cried Wolf* and it's about a clever lamb who is looked after by a very silly boy. I think you might want to check that book out, too!

MONSTER: Thank you, Lamb. I am so lucky having friends who read! That sounds like a very good book … *The Boy Who Cried Wolf*.

LAMB: Have a good time at the library, Monster. I have to go now.

(LAMB exits the stage.)

MONSTER: (trying very hard to concentrate) Now I have two books to remember: *The Three Little Pigs* and *The Boy Who Cried Wolf*. I hope I can remember all that! (looks offstage toward the direction of FOX) Look, there's my friend Fox! Hello, Fox. (to the audience) This must be my lucky day—seeing so many of my friends.

(FOX enters the stage.)

FOX: Hello, Monster. How are you today?

MONSTER: Just fine, thank you. I am on my way to the library to check out some good books. Pig told me about a book called *The Three Little Pigs* and Lamb told me about a book called *The Boy Who Cried Wolf*. So now I have two good books to ask for!

FOX: (disgusted) Leave it to Pig and Lamb to suggest such wimpy books! I know a story you'll really like! It's called *The Gingerbread Man* and it's about a tricky fox who fools a gingerbread man and ends up eating him! Now, that's *my* idea of a good book!

MONSTER: Thank you, Fox. That does sound good ... violent but good ... *The Gingerbread Man*.

FOX: All this talk of gingerbread men is making me hungry. I'm going to get something to eat. I'll see you later, Monster.

(FOX exits the stage.)

MONSTER: (trying even harder to concentrate) Now I have three books to remember: *The Three Little Pigs, The Boy Who Cried Wolf,* and *The Gingerbread Man*! (exhausted from too much concentration) Whew! I hope I can remember them all when I get to the library!

(MONSTER exits the stage, mumbling the titles of the books very quietly to himself.)

SCENE TWO: (After a few seconds, MONSTER enters the stage from the opposite side from which he exited.)

MONSTER: (looking around him) Here I am at the library! (inhales deeply, sniffing) HHHhhhmmmmmm. (to the audience) Don't these books smell delicious? This is so exciting—I have never had three books to find before. Maybe I should ask the librarian to help me. (looks offstage toward the direction of the LIBRARIAN) Excuse me, Librarian, I need some help finding books.

(LIBRARIAN enters the stage.)

LIBRARIAN: Hello, Monster, it's nice to see you again. How can I help you?

MONSTER: (eagerly) I want to find three books!

LIBRARIAN: Just tell me the names of the three books and I'll be happy to help you find them.

MONSTER: (slightly confused) Names? Let's see, they were all pretty long. Let me think for a minute. (MONSTER strikes a "thinking" posture then suddenly remembers.) I remember now! The books were *The Three Little Wolves, The Boy Who Cried Man*, and *The Gingerbread Pigs!* (proud of himself) So, where can I find them?

LIBRARIAN: (perplexed) I've never heard of any books with those titles. Are you sure you have the correct names?

MONSTER: (determined) Of course! The books I want are *The Three Little Boys, The Man Who Cried Pig*, and *The Gingerbread Wolf*! (confused) No, that's not right.

LIBRARIAN: (understanding what MONSTER is looking for now) I think I know just what you're looking for: *The Three Little Pigs, The Boy Who Cried Wolf*, and *The Gingerbread Man*.

MONSTER: (delighted) Yes, yes, those were the books I wanted!

LIBRARIAN: Just follow me and I'll show you where they are.

(LIBRARIAN exits the stage.)

MONSTER: (to the audience and awestruck) Gee, that librarian sure is smart! I can't wait to read those books. Maybe tomorrow my friends will tell me about more good books for me to read. Goodbye, everybody.

(MONSTER exits the stage.)

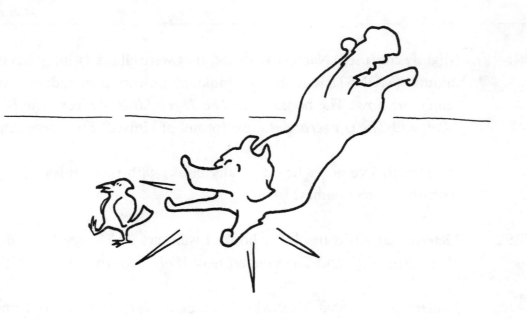

FOX LEARNS A LESSON

CHARACTERS: Pig (a likeable animal who loves to read)
Fox (a rather selfish creature who is more concerned with food than books)
Bird (just minding his or her own business)

PROPS: A long narrow strip of white fabric for the puppeteer to wrap around FOX's head as a bandage.

(PIG enters the stage, very excited.)

PIG: Hi, everybody! Boy, am I ever glad to be here! I've just read the greatest book. (PIG talks briefly to the audience about a book—possibly one which has just been shared together.) (PIG looks offstage) Hey, here comes Fox. I'll bet he'd like to hear about this book, too!

(FOX enters the stage.)

PIG: Hi there, Fox.

FOX: Hello, Pig.

PIG: Fox, I was just telling the kids about this great book I read. Maybe you'd like to hear about it, too. You see, it was all about—

FOX: (cutting PIG off in mid-sentence) I don't care about your silly books. Books are stupid! I have better things to do with my time than read silly books!

PIG: Well, I don't think books are silly at all! I love to read! There's so many different kinds of books to choose from ... why, I can read adventure stories or science fiction or funny stories. And of course, I love to read nonfiction books! Gosh, I've learned a lot of great things from reading books.

FOX: (unconvinced) Like what?

PIG: Well, I learned to bake chocolate chip cookies from a cookbook, and I learned to make a coin disappear from reading a book of magic tricks.

FOX: (unimpressed) Big deal!

PIG: Gosh, I'm sorry you don't like to read, Fox. You're really missing out on a lot of fun. I'm on my way to the library. I'll see you later.

(PIG exits the stage.)

FOX: That Pig is so boring! All he ever does is read. I don't like to read—it's just too hard. Anyway, I'd rather do other things ... like eat! That's a good idea, it's almost lunch time. Let's see, what should I have for lunch? (FOX leisurely looks about the stage—behind, underneath, and to either side. Suddenly, FOX sees BIRD offstage. FOX stares offstage in the direction from which BIRD will enter.) There's my lunch! I see a nice, juicy, plumb bird coming this way. I'll just hide myself over in that corner until that bird wanders by ... then, lunchtime!

(Chuckling to himself, FOX saunters to the far side of the stage and waits impatiently for BIRD to appear. BIRD pops up on the opposite side of the stage from FOX.)

BIRD: Cheep, cheep.

(BIRD slowly hops toward the center of the stage, as if pecking the ground. FOX very slowly creeps closer and closer until he lunges at BIRD, who quickly hops away in time to avoid FOX. BIRD excitedly hops away offstage and exits.)

FOX: (angrily) I could have caught that bird! I was just too weak from hunger, that's all! I'm going to catch that bird next time, you'll see. (FOX stalks back to the far side of the stage.) I'm going to wait right here for that bird to come back. (FOX looks to the opposite side of the stage, waiting for BIRD to appear.)

(BIRD pops up on the opposite side of the stage from FOX.)

BIRD: Cheep, cheep.

(BIRD once again slowly hops toward the center of the stage, as if pecking the ground. FOX very slowly creeps closer and closer until he lunges at BIRD, who once again quickly hops away in time to avoid FOX. BIRD very excitedly hops away offstage and exits.)

FOX: (livid with anger) So help me, I'm going to catch that bird if it's the last thing I ever do! I'm going back to that corner and wait!

(FOX stomps back to the far side of the stage, mumbling about what he's going to do to the bird.)

FOX: (through clenched teeth) Here, birdie ... nice birdie!

(BIRD pops up on the opposite side of the stage from FOX.)

BIRD: Cheep, cheep.

(BIRD once again slowly hops toward the center of the stage, as if pecking the ground. FOX very slowly creeps closer and closer until he makes a gigantic lunge at BIRD, who once again very quickly hops away in time to avoid FOX. BIRD excitedly hops away offstage and exits. This time FOX has hurt himself and he begins howling in pain.)

FOX: (crying and moaning) OOOOOooooohhhhHHHHH! My head is broken. I think I'm going to die! OOOOooooohhhhHHHHH!

(PIG enters the stage.)

PIG: (to the audience, not yet seeing FOX) What is that horrible noise? (sees FOX) What happened, Fox?

FOX: (sobbing) I fell and hurt my head. I think I killed myself. Can you help me, Pig?

PIG: I don't know for sure. I'd have to see how badly you're hurt. (PIG closely examines FOX's head.)

FOX: I'm really sorry for all those nasty things I said about books. I didn't mean them. Oh, my head! Please help me, Pig.

PIG: Well, I'll try. I was just reading a book all about first aid. Come along with me and I'll clean your wound and then bandage it. (PIG begins exiting offstage but turns back to fetch FOX.)

FOX: (cautiously) Are you sure you know what you're doing? You aren't going to hurt me, are you?

PIG: Trust me, Fox. You'll be okay—just come along with me, and I'll get you patched up.

(PIG and FOX exit the stage together. Once offstage, FOX's wails and moans can be heard while he is having the bandage put on his head. After a few moments, PIG and FOX return onstage with FOX wearing the white bandage.

FOX: (weakly) Are you sure I'm going to live?

PIG: Of course! All you need to do is keep ice on your head tonight to reduce the swelling.

FOX: (softening in his attitude toward PIG) Pig, I'm really sorry for all those rotten things I said about books and reading. You see, reading is awfully hard for me. I'm just not good at it. That's why I made fun of you.

PIG: Gee, I'm glad you told me, Fox. I'm not mad at you. In fact, I want to help you. I've got a great idea! How would you like to go with me to the library tomorrow? I know some books you'd really enjoy reading, and I promise they won't be too hard for you.

FOX: (still playing the invalid) I'd like to ... that is, *if* I'm feeling better.

PIG: I'm sure you will be. Just keep putting ice on your head tonight, and you'll be fine. I'll see you tomorrow. Goodbye, Fox. (to the audience) I guess Fox isn't so bad after all.

(PIG exits the stage.)

FOX: (calling offstage to PIG) Goodbye and thanks for your help. (to the audience) Maybe books aren't as silly as I thought. I wonder if the library will have any books on how to catch birds? Goodbye, everybody. See you at the library!

(FOX exits the stage.)

TAKE ME TO YOUR LIBRARY

CHARACTERS: Space Creature (a frightened visitor from the planet Orthon)
Pig (a likeable animal who loves to read)

PROPS: Several small "books" (which may be made by folding small sheets of paper with the covers made to resemble actual books).

(The stage is empty. Once in a while, there is a "beep-beep" noise that seems to be coming from offstage. Very slowly, SPACE CREATURE peeks its head onstage and emits a few "beep-beeps." Afraid, SPACE CREATURE quickly pops down below the stage level. This continues several more times until SPACE CREATURE gathers enough courage to emerge fully onstage.)

SPACE CREATURE: (to himself and not fully aware of the audience) I wonder if there is intelligent life on this remote planet called Earth? I do hope these Earthlings are friendly? I wonder what these Earthlings will look like. I am sure they are not as handsome as we Orthonites! I had better prepare myself for anything!

(SPACE CREATURE exits the stage. An occasional "beep-beep" is still heard coming from offstage, as if SPACE CREATURE is close by. After a few moments, PIG enters the stage.)

PIG: (to the audience and totally unaware of SPACE CREATURE's existence) Hi, everybody! I'm on my way to the library. They're having a special program there today, about stamp collecting. I'd like to stay and talk but I really should be going.

(Offstage, the "beep-beep" begins again, very loudly.)

PIG: (hearing the "beep-beep") What's that noise? Gee, it doesn't sound like anything I've ever heard before. (to the audience) Do any of you know what could be making that noise? (waits for a response from the audience) A what? A space creature from the planet Orthon? (not believing a word of it) Sure! Come on! All of you are just trying to kid me, right? We all know there are no such things as space creatures! I bet some little animal is making that noise, like a bird or a guinea pig. (still not believing) A space creature! I'm going to try finding that animal and see if it's hurt or needs help. Gosh, all of you must think I was born yesterday! A space creature!

(PIG exits the stage. After a few seconds, SPACE CREATURE once again appears, making its "beep-beep" noise. SPACE CREATURE is examining every inch of the stage for intelligent life. While SPACE CREATURE has its back toward center stage, PIG enters the stage, looking for the little animal he assumes is making the "beep-beep" noise. PIG enters the stage with his back toward center stage also. Now, the two characters slowly move closer together, still ignorant of the other's existence. Finally, they bump into each other. Both SPACE CREATURE and PIG scream in fright and exit the stage in opposite directions.)

PIG: (peeking his head onstage and to the audience) All of you were right! There really are such things as space creatures! (entering the stage) I guess that space creature was just as afraid of me as I was of it! I really should try to make contact with it. (calling offstage, toward the direction of SPACE CREATURE) Space Creature! You can come out now. I'm not going to hurt you! I just want to be friends!

(SPACE CREATURE very cautiously enters the stage, still very afraid.)

SPACE CREATURE: (to the audience) This Earthling is even uglier than I thought would be possible! I wonder if it will understand my language? (to PIG) Excuse me, are you an Earthling?

PIG: (to the audience) It's talking to me! It sounds like English! Maybe this space creature wants to be friends after all! (to SPACE CREATURE) Hello! Yes, I am an Earthling. Actually, I'm a pig. What planet did you come from?

SPACE CREATURE: (less afraid now) My planet is called Orthon and I come in peace. My mission is to examine your Earth and to take samples of what I find back to Orthon for study.

PIG: (astonished) Gee, this is all so unbelievable! And to think that I was just on my way to the library to see a program and get some books to read!

SPACE CREATURE: (interrupting PIG) Excuse me, Earthling. I am not familiar with three words you just used. What are "library," "books," and "read"?

PIG: (amazed) Gosh, don't you have those things on your planet?

SPACE CREATURE: No. Please explain them to me.

PIG: (perplexed) Gee, I really don't know how to explain "books" to you. You see, books are how we learn things and one way we entertain ourselves. And we do that through reading. And libraries are places where they have books and other great stuff. (sees that SPACE CREATURE is still confused) Golly, I guess I'm not making much sense. (has an idea) I know! I have some library books in my backpack right over there. I'll just go get them and show you what books are. I'll be back real soon!

(PIG exits the stage but returns shortly with several "books" which he sets onstage.)

PIG: (triumphantly) Here they are! These are books. See, these are words and here are some drawings. This is how we Earthlings learn things and read stories and have fun.

SPACE CREATURE: (impressed) Fascinating things, these books! They are much more interesting than the information chips we use on my planet. My mission is now complete! I have found the best possible things to take back to Orthon! I have found the best possible things to take back to Orthon! May I have these books to take with me back to Orthon and show my people? Perhaps we will be able to have books, too!

PIG: (hesitating) I don't know if I should. You see, those are library books, and I'm not supposed to let anything happen to them. Is it really so important for you to take these books right now?

SPACE CREATURE: (urgently) Oh, yes! I must hurry back to Orthon with these wonderful things called books!

PIG: Well, if it's so important, I guess you can take them with you. I don't suppose you could return them in a week? You see, that's when they're due back at the library!

SPACE CREATURE: I am afraid not, Earthling. Orthon is several galaxies away, and it takes several of your years to reach it.

PIG: In that case, take the books with you. I hope you'll enjoy books on Orthon as much as we do here on Earth!

SPACE CREATURE: (thankfully) We will never forget you and your great gift to Orthon! Thank you, Earthling, and goodbye!

(SPACE CREATURE exits with the books.)

PIG: (to the audience) Boy, just wait until I tell all my friends about this! The only bad thing is that I don't know how I'm ever going to convince the librarian that I gave my library books to a space creature! I guess I'd better start saving my allowance so I can pay for those library books! Goodbye, everybody!

(PIG exits the stage.)

DRAGON DRAWS A PICTURE

CHARACTERS: Pig (a likeable animal who is trying to tell the audience about the proper care of library books)
Dragon (his friend who unknowingly irritates Pig)

PROPS: A piece of paper, a crayon, a box of watercolors, and DRAGON's finished picture (which is on the same size and color as the first piece of paper).

(PIG enters the stage.)

PIG: (to the audience) Hi, everybody! Today, the librarian asked me to talk to all of you about how to take care of library books. I really don't know why she asked me. I guess it must be because I've been using the library for a long time. As a matter of fact, I've been using the library ever since I was a tiny piglet.

(DRAGON enters the stage.)

DRAGON: (to PIG) Excuse me, Pig. I don't want to disturb you when you're talking to the kids but could I borrow a piece of paper?

PIG: Sure, Dragon. (to the audience) Excuse me while I go get a piece of paper for Dragon.

(PIG exits the stage but returns shortly with a "piece of paper.")

PIG: Here you go, Dragon.

DRAGON: (taking the piece of paper) Thanks a lot.

(DRAGON exits the stage with the piece of paper.)

PIG: (to the audience) Let's see, what was I saying? Oh, I remember. I was telling you about how to care for library books. I learned a long time ago how important it is to take good care of library books. You see, one time I was reading while I was at the trough eating. You can imagine how messy we pigs tend to be when we eat! My library book had food stuck all over it and believe me, it was disgusting! I felt so bad because now that book was ruined and nobody else could read it. Also, I had to pay for a new copy of that book and it was pretty expensive! Why, I had to save my allowances for....

(DRAGON enters the stage, interrupting PIG in mid-sentence.)

DRAGON: (to PIG) Excuse me, Pig. Could I borrow a crayon?

PIG: Sure, Dragon. (to the audience) If you'll excuse me one more time, I'll go get a crayon for Dragon.

(PIG exits the stage but returns shortly with a "crayon.")

PIG: Here you go, Dragon.

DRAGON: (taking the crayon from PIG) Thanks a lot.

(DRAGON exits the stage with the crayon.)

PIG: (to the audience) Sorry for that interruption. As I was saying, I learned a long time ago how important it is to take good care of library books. Why, I remember one time I was reading this really great library book and the story was so good, I couldn't put it down—I just had to find out what happened! Well, I made the mistake of reading that book while I was taking a bath, and I accidently dropped it in the mud! Boy, that was an expensive book! I was washing windows for weeks to pay for that book!

(DRAGON once again enters the stage, interrupting PIG.)

DRAGON: (to PIG) Excuse me, Pig. Could I borrow your box of watercolors?

PIG: (getting irritated) Dragon, can't you see I'm busy talking to the kids?

DRAGON: Sorry to disturb you. The picture I'm drawing really needs some watercolors.

PIG: Okay, I'll go get them. (to the audience) Sorry about this.

(PIG exits the stage but returns shortly with the "box of watercolors.")

PIG: Here you go, Dragon. And I would really appreciate it if you didn't bother me anymore!

DRAGON: (taking the box of watercolors from PIG) Sure. Thanks a lot, Pig.

(DRAGON exits the stage with the box of watercolors.)

PIG: (to the audience) I'm *so* sorry that Dragon keeps interrupting us that way. You know, Dragon can be really thoughtless sometimes! Well, getting back to what I was talking about. I remember one time my little brother grabbed one of my library books and started drawing all over it! Gosh, was I ever mad at him! But at least that taught me always to put my library books in a special place where my little brother can't get to them. And of course I've learned never to eat while I'm reading or to take a bath while I'm reading. It's sure given me a lot more spending money!

(DRAGON enters the stage.)

DRAGON: (to PIG) Pig, I hate to bother you again, but I want to show you something.

PIG: (angrily) Dragon, how many times do I have to tell you to stop bothering me? First you borrow all my stuff and now you want to show me something! Dragon, please leave me alone!

DRAGON: (apologetically) I'm really sorry to keep bothering you, Pig. The picture I drew was of you and I wanted you to see it.

PIG: (surprised) Of me?

DRAGON: Sure. After all, you're my best friend. I'll go get it right now.

(DRAGON exits the stage.)

PIG: (to the audience) I feel like a real swine! All the time I was getting mad at Dragon, he was drawing a picture of *me*!

(DRAGON returns onstage with his "finished picture.")

DRAGON: (proudly) Here it is! What do you think?

PIG: (touched) It's the most beautiful picture I've ever seen, Dragon. I'm sorry that I got mad at you just now.

DRAGON: That's okay, Pig. I understand. You're still my best friend.

PIG: (to the audience) Well, I guess that's all I have to say about taking care of library books. I hope you all learned something—I know that I sure did. I learned that I have a very good friend in Dragon! Goodbye, everybody.

DRAGON: (to the audience) Goodbye.

(PIG and DRAGON exit the stage together with the finished picture.)

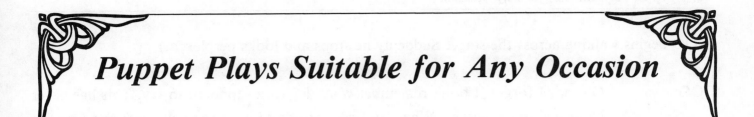

Puppet Plays Suitable for Any Occasion

THE DOG WHO FORGOT

CHARACTERS: Dog (a slightly forgetful animal)
Pig, Turkey, Mouse, and Boy (friends of Dog who try to help him remember)

(DOG enters the stage, yawning.)

DOG: (to the audience) What a beautiful morning. The sun is shining and the birds are singing. I think I'll go for a walk and visit some of my friends.

(DOG begins walking across the stage. Suddenly he stops and looks perplexed.)

DOG: Oh, no. I forgot. I don't remember what dogs are supposed to say. This has never happened to me before. What am I going to do? I better go ask my friend Pig. Pig knows everything. I'm sure he'll be able to help me. (calling offstage) Pig, Pig!

(PIG enters the stage.)

PIG: Hello, Dog. What's the matter?

DOG: (morosely) I'm in awful trouble, Pig. I woke up this morning and I forgot what it is that dogs are supposed to say. You've got to help me. Please?

PIG: Oh, that's easy. Dogs are supposed to say, "oink, oink."

DOG: (uncertain about this) Are you sure?

(PIG enthusiastically nods his head.)

DOG: Okay, here goes. "OINK, OINK, OINK." No, I don't think that's right. I think I would remember if I were supposed to say "oink, oink." Thanks anyway, Pig.

PIG: Goodbye, Dog, and good luck remembering.

(PIG exits the stage.)

DOG: (unhappily) What am I going to do? I've got to find out what I'm supposed to say. (has an idea) Maybe my friend turkey will know. Turkey is pretty smart. (calling offstage) Turkey, Turkey!

(TURKEY enters the stage.)

TURKEY: Hello, Dog. What's the matter?

DOG: (morosely) I'm in awful trouble, Turkey. I woke up this morning and I forgot what it is that dogs are supposed to say. You've got to help me. Please?

TURKEY: Oh, that's easy. Dogs are supposed to say, "gobble, gobble."

DOG: (confused) Are you sure?

(TURKEY enthusiastically nods her head.)

DOG: Okay, here goes. "GOBBLE, GOBBLE, GOBBLE." No, I don't think that's right. I think I would remember if I were supposed to say "gobble, gobble." Thanks anyway, Turkey.

TURKEY: Goodbye, Dog, and good luck remembering.

(TURKEY exits the stage.)

DOG: (very unhappily and to the audience) What's going to happen to me? I simply *have* to find out what I'm supposed to say. (has another idea) Maybe my friend Mouse will help me. (calling offstage) Mouse, Mouse!

(MOUSE enters the stage.)

MOUSE: Hello, Dog. What's the matter?

DOG: (morosely) I'm in awful trouble, Mouse. I woke up this morning and I forgot what it is that dogs are supposed to say. You've got to help me. Please?

MOUSE: Oh, that's easy. Dogs are supposed to say, "squeak, squeak."

DOG: (still confused) Are you sure?

(MOUSE enthusiastically nods his head.)

DOG: Okay, here goes. "SQUEAK, SQUEAK, SQUEAK." I don't think that's right. I think I would remember if I were supposed to say "squeak, squeak." Thanks anyway, Mouse.

MOUSE: Goodbye, Dog, and good luck remembering.

(MOUSE exits the stage.)

DOG: (almost crying) Just wait until all my friends see me. When they find out I forgot what dogs are supposed to say, they'll make fun of me.

(BOY enters the stage.)

BOY: (to DOG) What's the matter, Dog? You look upset.

DOG: (miserably) I'm in awful trouble. I woke up this morning and I forgot what it is that dogs are supposed to say.

BOY: I think I can help you.

DOG: (excited) You can? Really?

BOY: Sure. Dogs are supposed to sound like this. (BOY makes all kinds of dog-type noises: barks, woofs, and bow-wows.)

DOG: I remember now! (DOG barks, woofs, and bow-wows.) I don't know how I could have forgotten such a simple thing! Silly me! (to BOY) Thank you so much.

BOY: You're welcome. I'm just glad I was able to help. Are you sure you'll remember what you're supposed to say?

DOG: Of course! I'm never going to forget again!

BOY: Goodbye, Dog.

(BOY exits the stage.)

DOG: (to the audience) Now that I've remembered, I'm never going to forget!

(DOG begins walking across the stage. Suddenly he stops and looks perplexed.)

DOG: Oh, no. I forgot. (to the audience) Could you remind me just one more time what it is that I'm supposed to say? (DOG waits for the audience to bark, woof, and bow-wow.) Okay, okay. I remember now. Goodbye, everybody, and thanks for all your help.

(DOG exits the stage, barking, woofing, and bow-wowing.)

THE DRAGON HUNT

CHARACTERS: King (someone who has very firm ideas on how a prince should behave)
Prince (his son who has his own ideas)
Monster and Frog (two animals the Prince meets on his hunt)
Dragon (not the ferocious type found in stories)

SCENE ONE: (KING enters the stage.)

KING: (pacing the stage, very annoyed) Where is that son of mine? He was supposed to be here fifteen minutes ago! I don't know what to do about that boy! He just doesn't act like a prince is supposed to!

(PRINCE runs onstage.)

PRINCE: (out of breath) I'm sorry I'm so late, Father. I was feeding the birds and I guess I lost track of time.

KING: (frustrated) That's what I mean! You never act like a Prince! Whoever heard of a prince spending all of his time feeding birds and playing with animals?

PRINCE: (confused) Well, how is a prince supposed to act?

KING: A prince does princely sorts of things like save princesses and hunt down ferocious dragons. That's the reason I sent for you. The people in my kingdom are beginning to talk, so I want you to go on a dragon hunt. Bring back a ferocious, man-eating, fire-breathing dragon. Then everybody will know that you're a *real* prince!

PRINCE: (still confused) But I don't even know what a dragon looks like!

KING: (annoyed) Nonsense! Everyone knows that dragons are big and scary!

PRINCE: (being a good sport) Okay, I'll do my best.

(PRINCE exits the stage.)

KING: (to the audience) That boy had better bring back a dragon—or else!

(KING exits the stage.)

SCENE TWO: (PRINCE enters the stage.)

PRINCE: (to the audience) I've been wandering around now for nearly an hour and I still haven't found a dragon! My father said dragons are big and scary. If they are, I almost hope that I *don't* meet one!

(MONSTER enters from the opposite side of the stage.)

PRINCE: (to the audience) I wonder if that's a dragon? He's big and he's kind of scary. I hope he doesn't hurt me. (to MONSTER) Excuse me, but I was wondering something. Are you a dragon?

MONSTER: (surprised) Me? Oh, no, I'm not a dragon! I'm a monster. Dragons are big and scary and green!

PRINCE: Have you ever seen a dragon?

MONSTER: (shaking his head) No, but I've heard about them in stories!

PRINCE: I'm on a dragon hunt and I have to bring one back to my father.

MONSTER: Good luck! I'm glad that I'm not in your shoes!

(MONSTER exits the stage.)

PRINCE: (unhappily) Why was I ever born a prince? (sighs) I'd better keep looking for a dragon!

(FROG enters from the opposite side of the stage.)

PRINCE: (to the audience) I wonder if *that's* a dragon? She's not very big, and she's really isn't scary, but she *is* green! I'm sure she won't hurt me. (to FROG) Excuse me, but I was wondering something. Are you a dragon?

FROG: (surprised) Me? Oh, no, I'm not a dragon. I'm a frog. Dragons are big and scary and green and they breathe fire!

PRINCE: Have you ever seen a dragon?

FROG: (shaking her head) No, but I've heard about them in stories!

PRINCE: I'm on a dragon hunt, and I have to bring a dragon back to my father.

FROG: Good luck! I'm sure glad that I'm not in your shoes!

(FROG exits the stage.)

PRINCE: (very unhappily) I wish I could go home right now! But I can't until I find a dragon, so I'd better keep looking.

(DRAGON enters from the opposite side of the stage.)

PRINCE: (to the audience) I wonder if that's a dragon? He's kind of big, and he's sort of scary, and he is green, but I can't tell from here whether he breathes fire. (to DRAGON) Excuse me, but I was wondering something. Are you a dragon?

DRAGON: Me? Of course I am!

PRINCE: What a relief! Gosh, you seem friendly, too!

DRAGON: Naturally I'm friendly. Why wouldn't I be?

PRINCE: You see, everybody told me dragons were scary and breathed fire and captured princesses and did all sorts of other horrible things!

DRAGON: (angrily) I really don't know how all those stories got started! They aren't true at all! But I guess everybody believes them just the same. So why are you looking for a dragon?

PRINCE: My father has sent me on a dragon hunt. I'm supposed to bring a dragon back home to prove that I'm really a prince and very brave. (has an idea) You wouldn't want to come home with me, would you? I live in a castle, and I promise I would take very good care of you!

DRAGON: Sure, that sounds like fun! I've always wanted to live in a castle.

PRINCE: Oh, but there's one more thing! My father will expect you to be a ferocious dragon.

DRAGON: I'm not ferocious at all. I don't even think I could be!

PRINCE: (has another idea) I know! Maybe these kids will help us. (to the audience) Would all of you help Dragon act ferocious? (waits for a response from the audience) Good! When I count to three, will all of you roar a loud and ferocious roar? Okay, here goes: one, two, three! (waits while audience roars) That's just great! Now, when Dragon meets my father, you can all help him be ferocious! (to DRAGON) Come along home with me and we'll give my father a good scare!

(PRINCE and DRAGON exit the stage together.)

SCENE THREE: (KING enters the stage.)

KING: (to the audience) That son of mine has been gone nearly a day. I certainly hope he brings home a ferocious dragon! (looking offstage, toward the direction of PRINCE) Good! Here he comes now!

(PRINCE enters the stage.)

PRINCE: (triumphantly) Well, I'm home and I've brought a dragon along!

KING: (delighted) That's wonderful! I can't wait to see the ferocious dragon.

PRINCE: I'll send the dragon in to meet you, Father.

(PRINCE exits the stage. After a few seconds, DRAGON enters the stage.)

KING: (impressed) This looks like a very ferocious dragon!

DRAGON: (to the audience) Ready? Here we go: one, two, three!

(DRAGON, along with the audience, roars a ferocious roar!)

KING: (frightened) Oh, no! The dragon is going to attack me! I'd better run for my life!

(KING runs offstage. After a few seconds, PRINCE enters the stage.)

PRINCE: (to the audience) That was just great! (to DRAGON) You were wonderful! I'm going to tell Father the truth now. I've made you a sandwich because I thought you might be hungry after all that roaring! It's in the dining hall, so go help yourself.

DRAGON: Thanks, I am kind of hungry. Gee, this sure is fun! I think I'm going to like living here!

(DRAGON exits the stage.)

PRINCE: (calling offstage, toward the direction of KING) The dragon's gone now! It's safe to come out, Father!

(KING enters the stage.)

KING: (still frightened) That dragon is just too ferocious! We'll have to kill him!

PRINCE: Father, I want to tell you the truth. That dragon isn't really ferocious at all! He's actually a very nice dragon. I asked all the kids to help Dragon roar so that it would scare you. I'm sorry to play such a mean trick on you but, after all, you wanted me to bring back a ferocious dragon!

KING: To be honest, Son, I'm glad that dragon isn't ferocious! Let the people in my kingdom think whatever they want to! I'm glad you're the way you are! Will you take me to meet that dragon?

PRINCE: Sure. Come with me. He's in the dining hall, eating a sandwich. (to the audience) I'm glad that I went on that dragon hunt. And thanks to all of you for helping Dragon! Goodbye, everybody!

(PRINCE and KING exit the stage together.)

ELEPHANT'S SNEEZE

CHARACTERS: Dog (an easy-going, likeable animal)
Elephant (Dog's friend who worries too much)
Clown (a slightly pompous character with a very hectic schedule)

PROPS: A small paper bag (which the puppeteer puts over Elephant's head during the play).

SCENE ONE: (DOG enters the stage.)

DOG: (excitedly) Hi, everybody! I'm so happy for my friend Elephant. He's always dreamed of being a circus elephant and now his dream might come true. Today he has an interview with the head clown from the circus. If the head clown likes him, then Elephant will be part of the circus! Elephant promised me that he'd stop by to see me on his way to the interview. I hope he hurries. I don't want him to be late for his interview.

(Offstage, there is a "knock" at the door.)

DOG: (to the audience) I hope that's Elephant. (looks offstage toward the direction of ELEPHANT) Come in!

(ELEPHANT enters the stage.)

ELEPHANT: (full of nervous energy and pacing back and forth) Gosh, Dog, I am so scared about this interview. I've been worrying about it all day. What will I do if the head clown doesn't ... AA-AA-AA-CH-OOOOO! (ELEPHANT lets out a loud sneeze) ... like me?

DOG: Just be yourself, Elephant, and he's sure to like you.

ELEPHANT: (not convinced) I don't know about ... AA-AA-AA-CH-OOOOO! (ELEPHANT lets out another loud sneeze) ... that. Why do I keep sneezing?

DOG: Maybe it's your nerves. I've heard about things like this happening when someone is really nervous. All you have to do is relax. Don't you think you should be going now? You don't want to be late for your interview!

ELEPHANT: (dejectedly walking offstage) Yeah, I'll see you later. I just hope I don't make a complete fool of myself.

(ELEPHANT exits the stage. After he exits, another loud sneeze is heard from offstage.)

DOG: (still looking offstage in the direction ELEPHANT exited and calling out after him.) Good luck, Elephant! Just keep telling yourself, "relax, relax." (to the audience) I sure hope everything works out for Elephant.

(DOG exits the stage.)

SCENE TWO: (CLOWN hurriedly enters the stage.)

CLOWN: (pacing back and forth across the stage, not liking to wait for anyone) Where is that Elephant? He was supposed to be here 30 seconds ago! I'm a very busy clown and I hate to be kept waiting!

(Offstage, there is a "knock" at the door.)

CLOWN: It's about time—that had better be Elephant! (calling offstage toward ELEPHANT) Come in!

(ELEPHANT meekly peeks his head onto the stage.)

ELEPHANT: Sorry I'm late, but I had a tough time finding your ... AA-AA-AA-CH-OOOOO! (ELEPHANT lets out another loud sneeze which sends him flying into CLOWN's office) ... office.

CLOWN: Well, you certainly are here now. Turn around so that I can get a better look at you.

(ELEPHANT slowly turns around so that CLOWN can see all sides of him.)

CLOWN: (very pleased) Yes, you'll work out perfectly. You'll be a great circus elephant! When can you start working?

ELEPHANT: (amazed) You really want me to be a circus ... AA-AA-AA-CH-OOOOO! (ELEPHANT lets out another loud sneeze) ... elephant?

CLOWN: Sure. If you don't mind my asking a personal question, why do you keep sneezing? Do you have a cold?

ELEPHANT: (shaking his head) No.

CLOWN: Could it be an allergy?

ELEPHANT: No. My friend Dog thinks it's just my nerves ... AA-AA-AA-CH-OOOOO! (ELEPHANT lets out another loud sneeze)

CLOWN: Well, as soon as you're through with those sneezes, come back and see me. Then we'll start training you for your new job. People don't want to pay money to see an elephant sneeze at the circus!

ELEPHANT: No. Don't worry, I'll stop sneezing right away. Thanks a lot. Goodbye.

(ELEPHANT exits the stage.)

CLOWN: (to the audience) I can't wait for Elephant to start—he'll be perfect! I just hope he can get rid of those sneezes. I can't worry about that now—I have lots of work to do!

(CLOWN hurriedly exits the stage.)

SCENE THREE: (DOG enters the stage.)

DOG: (nervously pacing back and forth across the stage) I hope Elephant's interview went okay. I've been worrying about him all afternoon.

(Offstage, there is a "knock" at the door.)

DOG: I hope that's Elephant. (looking offstage toward ELEPHANT) Come in!

(ELEPHANT enters the stage.)

DOG: (excitedly) Elephant, you're back. How did it go?

ELEPHANT: Good and bad.

DOG: (perplexed) What do you mean?

ELEPHANT: The head clown thought I was perfect for the job of circus elephant but I couldn't stop ... AA-AA-AA-CH-OOOOO! (ELEPHANT lets out another loud sneeze) ... sneezing, and unless I can stop sneezing, I don't get the job. Dog, what am I going to do?

DOG: (thinking of a plan) All we have to do is make you stop sneezing.

ELEPHANT: But how do we do that?

DOG: Last night I was reading a book where one of the characters wanted to stop hiccupping. She tried all sorts of cures. Maybe some of the things she tried might work for sneezing too!

ELEPHANT: I'll try ... AA-AA-AA-CH-OOOOO! (ELEPHANT lets out another loud sneeze) ... anything! What do we do first?

DOG: Try holding your breath. Ready?

ELEPHANT: (nodding his head) Yes.

DOG: Hold your breath until I count to ten. Here we go: 1 ... 2 ... 3 ... 4 ... 5 ... 6 ... 7 ... 8 ... 9 ... 10! You can breathe now.

ELEPHANT: (letting out a gush of air) Whew! I think it worked, I don't feel like I have to ... AA-AA-AA-CH-OOOOO! (ELEPHANT lets out another loud sneeze) ... sneeze. Oh, no!

DOG: Don't give up yet. I have another cure to try. In the book, the character stood on her head. Maybe that will work. Try to stand on your head, Elephant.

ELEPHANT: (uncertain about all of this) Okay. (After some effort, ELEPHANT manages to turn slightly upside-down.)

DOG: Just to be sure it works, why don't you hold your breath, too? Ready? Here we go: 1 ... 2 ... 3 ... 4 ... 5 ... 6 ... 7 ... 8 ... 9 ... 10! You can stand up and breathe now, Elephant.

ELEPHANT: (letting out a gush of air and righting himself) Whew! I'm sure it worked that time! I don't feel like I have to ... AA-AA-AA-CH-OOOOO! (ELEPHANT lets out another loud sneeze) ... sneeze. Oh, no!

DOG: Don't worry, there's still one more cure to try. All we need to do is put a paper bag on your head and hold your breath!

ELEPHANT: (in disbelief) What?

DOG: (explaining it very slowly) Put a paper bag on your head and hold your breath. I'll go get a paper bag right now.

(DOG exits the stage but returns shortly with a "small paper bag.")

DOG: Just put this bag over your head like this. (DOG, with the help of the puppeteer, places the opened bag over ELEPHANT's head.) Now, take a big breath and hold it until I count to ten. Ready?

ELEPHANT: (muffled from having the bag over his head) I guess so.

DOG: Here we go: 1 ... 2 ... 3 ... 4 ... 5 ... 6 ... 7 ... 8 ... 9 ... 10! You can breathe now, Elephant. How do you feel?

ELEPHANT: (still muffled) Not too bad. I think maybe my sneezing has ... AA-AA-AA-CH-OOOOO! (ELEPHANT sneezes the paper bag off his head. The paper bag should land behind the puppet stage, out of sight of the audience.) ... stopped. What am I going to do now, Dog? I just have to stop sneezing or I'll never be a circus elephant.

DOG: (sadly) Gosh, we've tried every idea I know. I just don't have any more answers. I guess we'll ... AA-AA-AA-CH-OOOOO! (DOG lets out a loud sneeze)

ELEPHANT: (surprised) What was that?

DOG: (just as surprised as ELEPHANT) I sneezed!

ELEPHANT: You know what, I don't feel like sneezing anymore. Hey, it worked! My sneezes have disappeared!

DOG: I'm glad your sneezes are gone, but now I think I have them … AA-AA-AA-CH-OOOOO! (DOG lets out a loud sneeze)

ELEPHANT: This is great! Now I can go see the head clown tomorrow and start my training as a circus elephant. And it's all because of you, Dog! And don't worry about your sneezes, I've got a great cure that's sure to work! (to the audience) Next time any of you go to the circus, be sure to look for me! Goodbye, everybody! Dog, let's go find that paper bag!

DOG: Goodbye … AA-AA-AA-CH-OOOOO! (DOG lets out a loud sneeze)

(ELEPHANT and DOG exit the stage together.)

THE MYSTERIOUS EGG

CHARACTERS: Fox (a greedy animal who is always thinking about eating)
                    Pig (a well-meaning creature who can't bear to see an egg abandoned)
                    Rabbit (just minding his or her own business)
                    Dinosaur (after hatching from its egg, a friendly creature)

PROPS: A puppet-sized basket containing a large plastic egg.

SCENE ONE: (FOX enters the stage.)

FOX: (to the audience) Hello, everybody. (looking around the stage) Is the coast clear? (waits for a response from the audience) Good! I'll be right back!

(FOX exits the stage but returns shortly with the "basket containing a large plastic egg" which he sets onstage.)

FOX: (to the audience) Today must be my lucky day! There I was, walking in the woods, looking for something tasty to eat. Then, I saw *this*! A basket with a beautiful egg in it. Gee, and it's not even Easter! I can't wait to eat this yummy egg!

RABBIT: (singing from offstage) La, la, la, la.

FOX: (perks up and listens) That sounds like a rabbit! (looks at basket) This egg can wait for later!

(RABBIT enters the stage.)

RABBIT: (not seeing FOX and still singing) La, la, la, la.

FOX: (to the audience) I think I'll have a rabbit for breakfast!

(FOX chases RABBIT offstage. The basket remains onstage alone. After a few seconds, PIG enters the stage.)

PIG: (to the audience) What a beautiful day for a walk! (sees basket onstage) I wonder what this basket is doing here? And there's an egg in it! (looks around the stage) I don't see anybody here. Gee, I can't go off and leave this egg all by itself! (has an idea) Maybe I'll take it home with me. That way, I can look for its mother or whoever it belongs to.

(PIG exits the stage with the basket. After a few seconds, FOX enters the stage.)

FOX: (angrily to the audience) Drat! I almost caught that rabbit but he was just too fast for me. Oh well, I've still got my nice little egg! (looking around the stage) It was right here! What happened to my egg? (to the audience) Do any of you know what happened to my egg? (waits for a response from the audience) Pig took it? I think I'll go find Pig right now!

(FOX storms offstage.)

SCENE TWO: (PIG enters the stage with the basket which he sets onstage.)

PIG: (exhausted) Whew! That basket sure is heavy! I don't think I've ever seen an egg like this before. It's too big to be a chicken egg, and I don't think it's a duck egg or even an ostrich egg. I wonder what kind of egg it is?

FOX: (from offstage) Hold it right there, Pig!

(FOX enters the stage.)

FOX: (angrily) I want that egg, Pig!

PIG: (confused) What are you talking about?

FOX: You've got my egg and I want it!

PIG: (still confused) How could I possibly have your egg? I happen to know that foxes don't lay eggs!

FOX: (trying to be sweet) I was baby-sitting it. Please give it back to me—its mother will be *so* worried!

PIG: (suspiciously) I don't know. I don't trust you, Fox. I'm going to take this egg home with me and keep it safe until I find who it belongs to.

FOX: (menacingly moving closer to PIG) Give me that egg!

PIG: No!

FOX: I mean it, Pig. I want that egg!

PIG: No!

FOX: Okay, you asked for it!

(FOX shoves PIG, causing the basket to fall behind the stage.)

PIG: (fed up with FOX's rude behavior) Now, see what you made me do! Sometimes you make me so mad, Fox! I only hope that egg is still in one piece!

(PIG runs offstage.)

FOX: (to the audience) Pig gets upset so easily! If that egg is still in one piece, I'll just wait for it to hatch—then I'll go pay a visit on my "friend" Pig! A "lunch" visit, you might say! (FOX laughs at his own joke.)

(FOX exits the stage.)

SCENE THREE: (PIG enters the stage.)

PIG: (out of breath) Whew! I got to that egg just in time! It's still in one piece, but there's a big crack going down one side of it!

(From offstage, comes a high-pitched "eep-eep" noise.)

PIG: (perplexed) What's that noise? (looking around the stage.) Maybe it's the egg! I'd better go check.

(PIG exits the stage. The "eep-eep" noise gets louder offstage. After a few seconds, PIG enters the stage.)

PIG: (in awe) It's hatched! And it isn't a chicken ... or a duck ... or even an ostrich! I don't know what it is! (to the audience) Maybe you'll know what it is. (looking offstage, toward the direction of DINOSAUR) Here it comes now!

(Slowly, DINOSAUR emerges from beneath the stage.)

DINOSAUR: Eep-eep!

PIG: (to the audience) What do you think it is? (waits for a response from the audience) A dinosaur? (to DINOSAUR) Are you a dinosaur?

DINOSAUR: (agreeing) Eep-eep!

PIG: Gosh, I don't know the first thing about taking care of a dinosaur! I don't even know what kind of food they eat! I'd better go to the library and get some books about dinosaurs. (to DINOSAUR) I'm going to the library and I'll be right back. While I'm gone, don't let anybody in and don't go outside. Do you understand?

DINOSAUR: (agreeing) Eep-eep!

PIG: See you soon.

(PIG exits the stage. For a few seconds, DINOSAUR is left alone onstage and then slowly exits offstage in the direction opposite of PIG.)

SCENE FOUR: (FOX enters the stage.)

FOX: (to the audience) It's time for lunch, and I'm in the mood for a tasty little chicken! I'm sure that egg has hatched by now! (calling offstage, toward the direction of DINOSAUR) Hello, little chicken! Come on out!

DINOSAUR: (from offstage) Eep-eep!

FOX: (to the audience) What a cute little voice! (calling offstage again) I've come to pay a visit to you, little chicken. I'm your Uncle Fox!

DINOSAUR: (still from offstage) Eep-eep!

FOX: (to the audience) Here it comes now—lunch!

(Very slowly, DINOSAUR emerges from beneath the stage.)

FOX: (astonished) What is it? (to the audience) Do you know what it is? (waits for a response from the audience) It's a dinosaur! I thought they were extinct! (very afraid and to DINOSAUR) You stay away from me, you dinosaur!

DINOSAUR: (coming closer to FOX) Eep-eep!

FOX: (terrified) Stay away from me! Don't come any closer to me! Aaaaahhh!

(FOX runs offstage, slowly followed by DINOSAUR.)

SCENE FIVE: (PIG enters the stage.)

PIG: (out of breath and to the audience) Golly, I just saw Fox running faster than I've ever seen him run before! I have a feeling that he met my dinosaur! Well, I sure hope Fox learns something from all of this. Maybe next time Fox finds an egg, he won't be in such a hurry to take it! By the way, I found out lots of neat things about dinosaurs at the library. I'd like to stay and talk but I'd better go feed my dinosaur right away! Goodbye, and thanks for helping me!

(PIG exits the stage.)

Part 3
Patterns for Puppets

Puppet Patterns

Here are patterns and directions for making five basic types of puppets. These patterns are very simple and should be easy for adults and children to construct. Young children will enjoy creating the paper-bag and stick puppets, while older children will turn their imaginations loose with the finger, hand, and mouth puppets. As always, please make certain that adults are supervising any necessary sewing of the puppets.

PAPER-BAG MOUTH PUPPETS

Paper-bag mouth puppets make an ideal follow-up activity for any of the puppet plays found in this book. Also, you'll discover that children need little coaxing to put on their own plays (with or without a stage) using these puppets.

These patterns are scaled to fit a paper lunch bag, which is approximately five by three by ten inches. These bags are available in either brown or white, and may be purchased inexpensively at any supermarket or discount store. Each puppet requires two pieces, which are designated "Piece A" and "Piece B." Piece A is the head of the puppet, and Piece B is the inside of the puppet's mouth. All you need to do to create a paper-bag mouth puppet is:

1. Photocopy Pieces A and B for each puppet.

2. Color each piece with crayons or markers.

3. Cut out both pieces.

4. Glue Piece B to the paper bag, as shown in Figure 9.

5. Glue Piece A to the bottom of the paper bag, as shown in Figure 10.

6. Let the pieces dry thoroughly to the paper bag.

To manipulate your paper-bag mouth puppet, place your hand into the still-closed bottom of the bag and make a gentle waving motion, moving your fingers away from the palm of your hand (see Figure 11). This motion causes your puppet to "talk."

Included here are patterns for Little Billy Goat Gruff, Middle Billy Goat Gruff, Big Billy Goat Gruff, Dragon, Elf, Fox, Leprechaun, Monster, Pig, Space Creature, and Troll (see Figs. 12-22).

For more ideas and patterns for paper-bag puppets, you may want to look in appendix B of this book, and especially at two books listed there: *Bagging It with Puppets* by Gloria Mehrens and Karen Wick, and *Paper-bag Puppets* by DeAtna M. Williams.

(Text continues on page 207.)

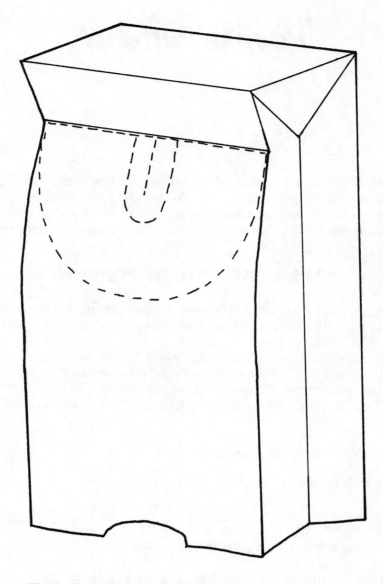

Fig. 9. Paper-bag mouth puppets

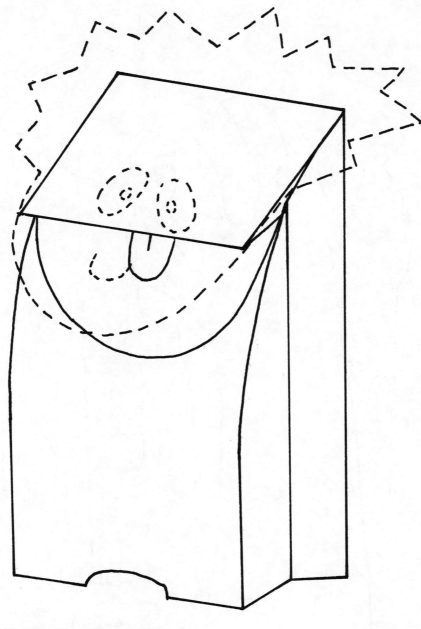

Fig. 10. Paper-bag mouth puppet

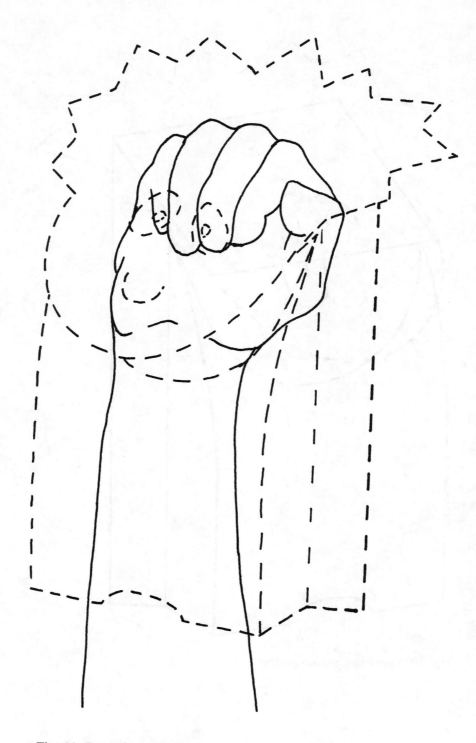

Fig. 11. Paper-bag mouth puppets

Piece A

Fig. 12a. Little Billy Goat Gruff paper-bag mouth puppet

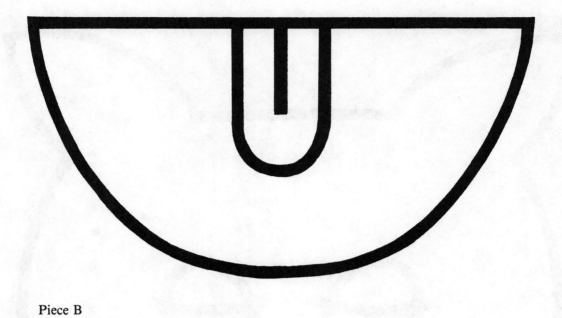

Piece B

Fig. 12b. Little Billy Goat Gruff paper-bag mouth puppet

Piece A

Fig. 13a. Middle Billy Goat Gruff paper-bag mouth puppet

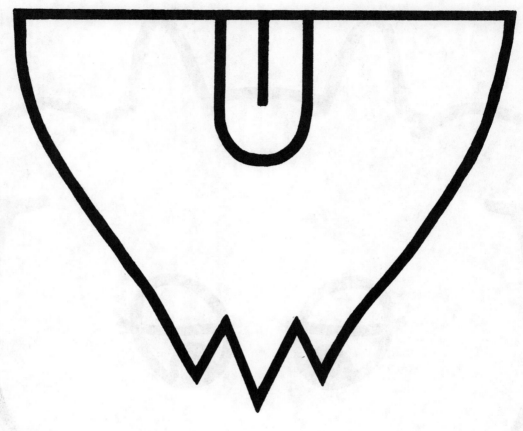

Piece B

Fig. 13b. Middle Billy Goat Gruff paper-bag mouth puppet

Piece A

Fig. 14a. Big Billy Goat Gruff paper-bag mouth puppet

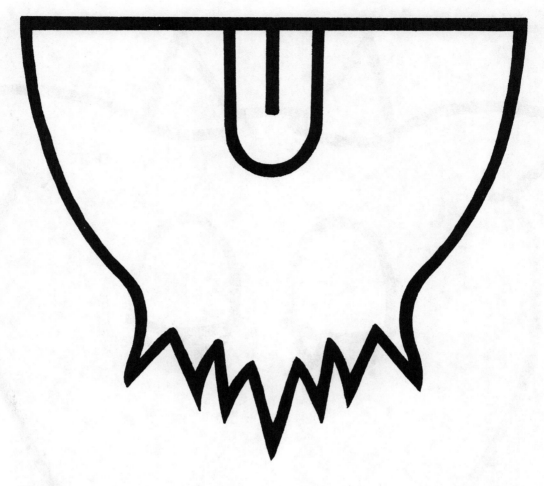

Piece B

Fig. 14b. Big Billy Goat Gruff paper-bag mouth puppet

Piece A

Fig. 15a. Dragon paper-bag mouth puppet

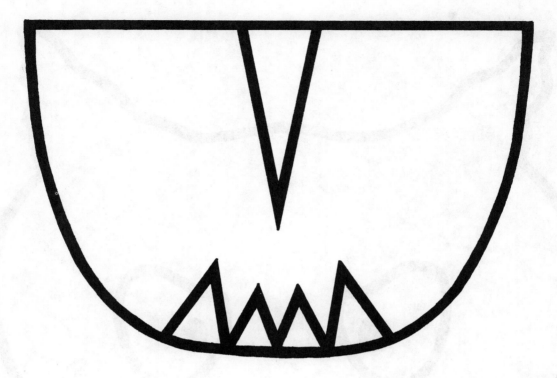

Piece B

Fig. 15b. Dragon paper-bag mouth puppet

Piece A

Fig. 16a. Elf paper-bag mouth puppet

Piece B

Fig. 16b. Elf paper-bag mouth puppet

Piece A

Fig. 17a. Fox paper-bag mouth puppet

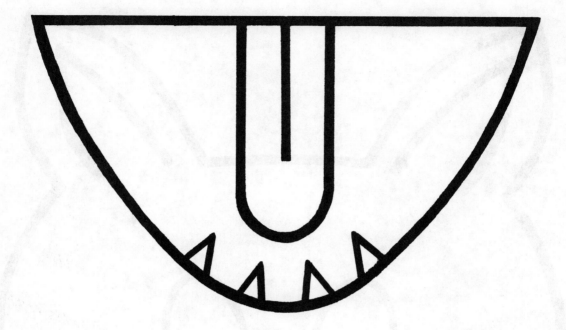

Piece B

Fig. 17b. Fox paper-bag mouth puppet

Piece A

Fig. 18a. Leprechaun paper-bag mouth puppet

Piece B

Fig. 18b. Leprechaun paper-bag mouth puppet

Piece A

Fig. 19a. Monster paper-bag mouth puppet

Piece B

Fig. 19b. Monster paper-bag mouth puppet

Piece A

Fig. 20a. Pig paper-bag mouth puppet

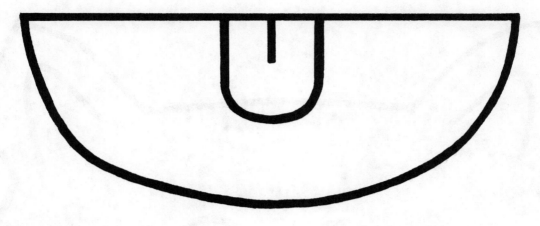

Piece B

Fig. 20b. Pig paper-bag mouth puppet

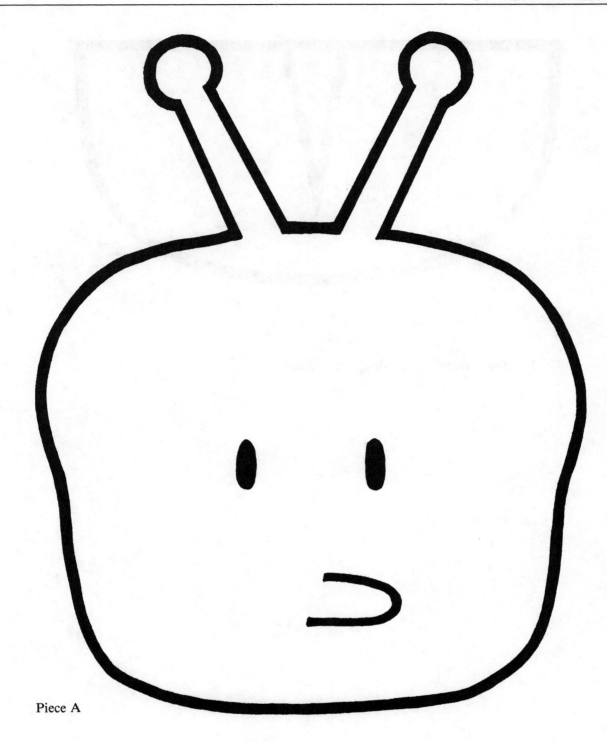

Piece A

Fig. 21a. Space creature paper-bag mouth puppet

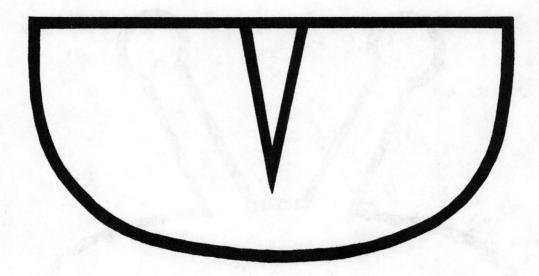

Piece B

Fig. 21b. Space creature paper-bag mouth puppet

Piece A

Fig. 22a. Troll paper-bag mouth puppet

Piece B

Fig. 22b. Troll paper-bag mouth puppet

STICK PUPPETS

By far the easiest puppets to make, stick puppets have uses both as a follow-up activity and as actual characters in several of the puppet plays contained in this book. Because of their small size and lack of moveable "hands" or "mouths," stick puppets are best suited for puppet characters which require little dialogue and very stylized movements. The six drawings included here are intended to serve as patterns for stick puppets that may be used as characters in my puppet plays or as follow-up activities for your audience. Characters from the preceding plays that work well as stick puppets are: Bat, Bird, Dinosaur, Johnny-cake, Mouse, and Turkey (see Figs. 23-28). All you need to do to create one of these stick puppets is:

1. Photocopy one of the accompanying patterns for stick puppets.

2. Color this pattern with crayons or markers.

3. Cut out the pattern.

4. Using glue, tape, or staples, attach the puppet character to a craft stick, narrow rod, or plastic drinking straw.

To manipulate your stick puppet, simply hold the puppet's stick and move the character according to the needs of the puppet play. Some suggestions for movements are: a gentle flying and hovering action for Bat, quick hopping and pecking motions for Bird, a low lumbering walk for Dinosaur, a fluid, rolling movement for Johnny-cake, quick, scurrying motions for Mouse, and a sharp, prancing action for Turkey. Try creating more stick puppets by photocopying some of the drawings in this book which feature a single character.

(Text continues on page 214.)

Fig. 23. Bat stick puppet

Fig. 24. Bird stick puppet

Fig. 25. Dinosaur stick puppet

Fig. 26. Johnny-cake stick puppet

Fig. 27. Mouse stick puppet

Fig. 28. Turkey stick puppet

SOME TIPS ON SEWING PUPPETS

The sewing required to make the following patterns for finger puppets, mouth puppets, and hand puppets can be done either by hand or by machine. Quarter-inch seam allowances are indicated for each pattern with segmented lines. Fabrics which may be used for these puppets include fake fur, velour, polyester knit, and felt. The fabric you choose will depend on the type of puppet character you are constructing and how much heavy use it will receive. If children will be the primary users of the puppet, durability and washability become important factors in the selection of fabric for puppet construction. If a puppet is going to be used primarily by adults in presenting puppet plays, these factors become less important. Fake furs work well for animal or monster puppets, and can be used as "hair" for human characters. In addition, fake fur is very durable and can be gently washed if care is taken in drying and restoring the appearance of the fur. Velour, polyester knit, and felt are suitable for human characters, but vary greatly in their durability and washability. Felt is easy to work with, but is the least durable of these fabrics, and requires great care in washing. Both velour and polyester knit are very durable and can be easily washed and dried.

Always use a sharp pair of sewing scissors when cutting the puppet pattern from fabric. Even when a pattern specifies "cut 2," it's a good idea to cut only one pattern piece at a time. This is especially true when working with fake furs, which have a tendency to shift. Also, when cutting fake fur, pin the pattern to the stiff cloth backing which is actually the wrong side of the fabric. Then, carefully cut only this backing and not the fur on the reverse side. Always be aware that fake furs have a distinct pile, which has a definite "up" and "down." The head, body, and arms of a puppet should have this fur pile running "down." Tails or ears are suitable for the fur pile running "up."

All the finishing details for these puppets are sewn by hand. These details may include adding eyes, ears, noses, or whiskers to the puppet. Eyes can be made from felt or sew-on "wiggle eyes," which are available in craft stores. Patterns for ears are included when needed for these puppets. Noses can be made by sewing small pom-poms on the puppet. If whiskers are needed, use a heavy quilting thread; a double strand of this thread is drawn through the nose area and then cut and knotted on either side of the puppet's nose. If you plan on constructing puppets on a regular basis, consider starting a scrap box filled with items you can use when making puppets. These items can include yarn pieces, felt scraps, pom-poms, wiggle eyes, and the like.

The following patterns are drawn to fit an adult's finger or hand. If you would like to use these patterns with children, all you need to do is reduce them on a photocopier until they are the suitable size.

FINGER PUPPETS

Here is a simple pattern for a finger puppet. Its use in puppet plays is rather limited, but finger puppets are well-suited to informal, small-group puppet presentations and individual use by children. In one-person puppet plays, finger puppets work best for characters which have limited dialogue and require a stylized movement such as Bird, Mouse, and Rabbit. Even with its shortcomings as a suitable fabric for puppet construction, felt works very well for these finger puppets. As you will notice, the patterns for ears, wings, and arms do not include a seam allowance (see Fig. 29). For the purposes of these three puppets, the appendages are simply cut from felt and sewn into the seam of the finger puppet body. All you need to do to create a finger puppet is:

1. Cut two of the "body" pattern.

2. Cut the required number of appendage pieces for each puppet.

3. Take one body piece; place the appendage pieces on the body but in the reverse position of where they will be on the finished puppet. Pin or baste these pieces in place.

4. Lay the second body piece over the first and carefully sew along the edge, using a quarter-inch seam allowance. Be certain to sew through any appendage pieces.

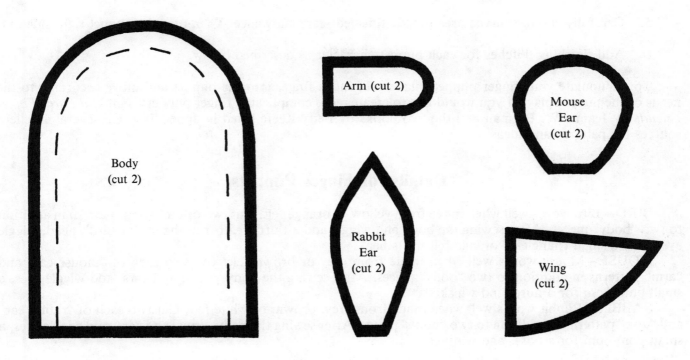

Fig. 29. Basic finger puppet pattern

5. Carefully clip the curved areas of the finished seam allowance. Then turn the puppet right side out.

6. Add finishing touches for each puppet character as described below.

To manipulate your finger puppet, place your index finger into the puppet and move according to the needs of the puppet play. If you would like to create more complicated finger puppets, *Fanciful Furry Finger Friends* by Jeanne W. Pittman and the two books by Betty Keefe listed in appendix B are several excellent sources for patterns and ideas.

Details for Finger Puppets

BIRD—Bird works well when made from yellow or orange felt. Cut two of the "wing" pattern in addition to two "body" pieces. After sewing the body and wings, add a fluffy feather at the top of Bird's head, wiggle eyes, and a small triangle of orange felt as its beak.

MOUSE—Mouse works well when made from grey or brown felt. Cut two each of "mouse ear" and "arm" patterns in addition to two "body" pieces. After sewing the body, arms, and ears, add wiggle eyes, a small pom-pom for a nose, and whiskers.

RABBIT—Rabbit works well when made from grey, brown, or white felt. Cut two each of "rabbit ear" and "arm" patterns in addition to two "body" pieces. After sewing the body, arms, and ears, add wiggle eyes, a small pom-pom for a nose, and whiskers.

MOUTH PUPPETS

Here are two simple patterns for mouth puppets, one with a rounded mouth (Figs. 30a and 30b, Pieces A and B), and the other featuring a pointed mouth (Figs. 31a and 31b, Pieces C and D). Animal characters work well as mouth puppets, and, by using both the rounded and pointed styles, a wide variety of animal puppets can be constructed. The rounded-mouth pattern suits Cat, Dog, Frog, Monster, Mouse, Rabbit, and Reindeer. The pointed-mouth pattern suits Crocodile, Dragon, Fox, Lion, Rat, and Wolf. Fabrics which work well with mouth puppets are fake fur, velour, and felt. All you need to do to create a mouth puppet is:

1. Cut two of Piece A (or C). If a longer puppet is desired, merely lengthen the bottom edge of the pattern. The large dot on either side of the curve on Piece A (or C) is the stopping point when sewing the "mouth" of the puppet. It is important to note these two dots on the fabric pieces either by placing a pin in that location or marking the fabric with dressmaker's chalk or thread.

2. Cut one of Piece B (or D) after placing it on the fold of your fabric.

3. With the right side of both fabric pieces together, pin or baste Piece A (or C) to Piece B (or D), matching the curved area. Sew along this curve to the large dot on either side of Piece A (or C).

4. When both fabric pieces of Piece A (or C) have been sewn to Piece B (or D) up to the large dot, the mouth portion of the puppet is complete.

5. Still keeping the right sides of the fabric together, sew the two side seams from the mouth portion to the bottom edge of the puppet.

6. After all the seams have been sewn, carefully clip the curved areas and turn the puppet right side out.

7. Add finishing touches for each puppet character.

(Text continues on page 226.)

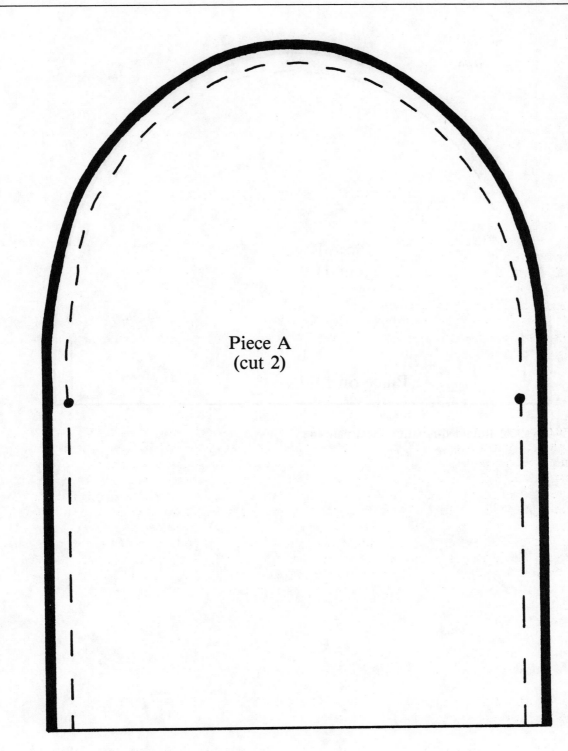

Fig. 30a. Rounded-mouth puppet pattern

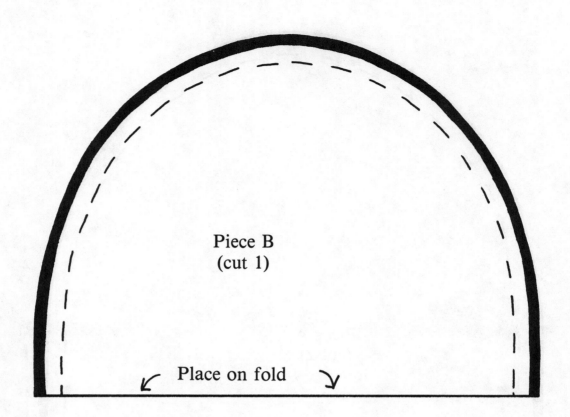

Fig. 30b. Rounded-mouth puppet pattern

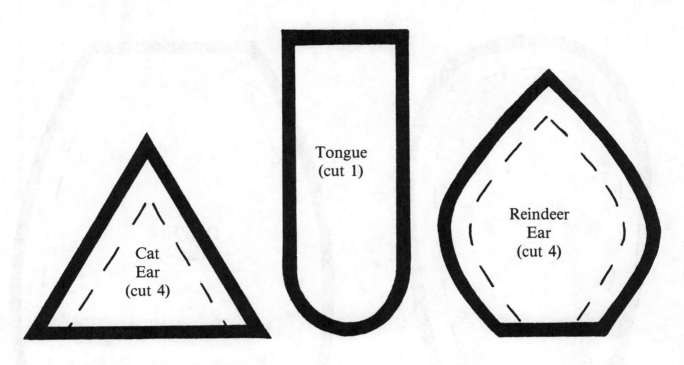

Fig. 30c. Rounded-mouth puppet pattern.

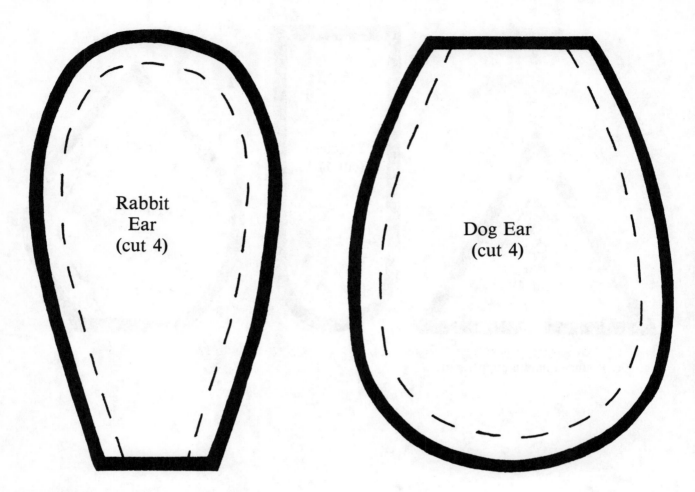

Rabbit
Ear
(cut 4)

Dog Ear
(cut 4)

Fig. 30d. Rounded-mouth puppet pattern

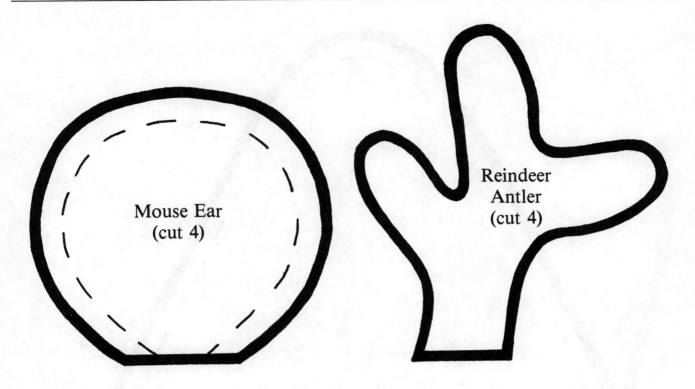

Mouse Ear
(cut 4)

Reindeer
Antler
(cut 4)

Fig. 30e. Rounded-mouth puppet pattern

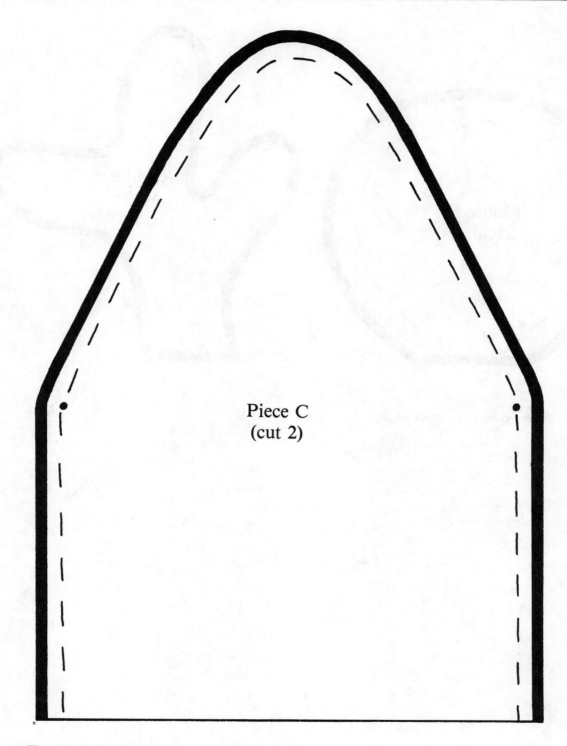

Piece C
(cut 2)

Fig. 31a. Pointed-mouth puppet pattern

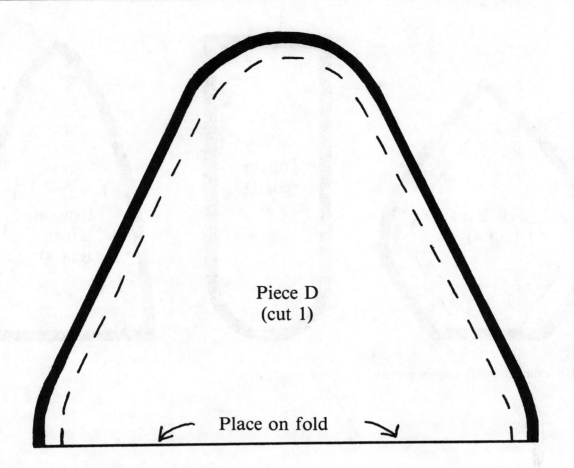

Piece D
(cut 1)

Place on fold

Fig. 31b. Pointed-mouth puppet pattern

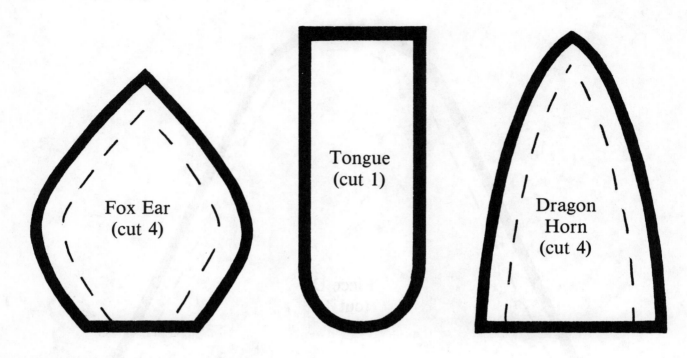

Fox Ear
(cut 4)

Tongue
(cut 1)

Dragon
Horn
(cut 4)

Fig. 31c. Pointed-mouth puppet pattern

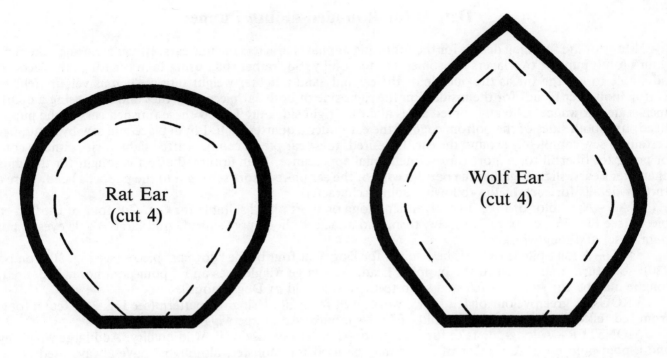

Fig. 31d. Pointed-mouth puppet pattern

Details for Rounded-mouth Puppets

Many of the finishing details for the following animal characters include ears. If you are using fake fur for your mouth puppet, two layers are sometimes too bulky. So, rather than using fake fur for both pieces, it is advisable to use the fur as the outside of the ear only and a lighter-weight fabric, such as velour, felt, or a cotton/polyester blend, for the inside. Pin the right side of both ear pieces together and sew, using a quarter-inch seam allowance. Clip any curved areas and turn right side out. To sew these finished ears to the puppet's head, turn both sides of the bottom edge of the ear under a quarter-inch. Pin in place and sew by hand, being certain to sew completely around the ear. If desired, these ear pieces can be stuffed lightly with either a cotton or polyester fiberfill for a more three-dimensional appearance. If an upturned effect is sought for the animal character's ears, slightly gather the bottom edge of the ear piece before sewing it to the puppet's head. Here are further details for each of the following animal characters.

CAT—Any color of fake fur with either a long or short pile is suitable for Cat. Cut four of the "cat ear" pieces (see Fig. 30c, on page 219); sew, turn, and attach to the puppet's head. Add large wiggle eyes, a pom-pom nose, and long whiskers.

DOG—A long-pile fake fur is best suited for Dog. Cut four of the "dog ear" pieces (see Fig. 30d, on page 220); sew, turn, and attach to the puppet's head. Add large wiggle eyes and a pom-pom nose. If desired, a tongue may be cut from red felt and sewn to the inside fold of Dog's mouth.

FROG—A green velour or felt fabric works well for Frog. Using the pattern (see Fig. 30c), cut a tongue from red felt and sew to the inside fold of Frog's mouth. Add large wiggle eyes.

MONSTER—A long-pile fake fur is ideal for Monster because of its wild quality. Add large wiggle eyes and a pom-pom nose. Any color of fabric may be used for Monster, although I have always used blue. If desired, a tongue, horns, or even antlers could be added to Monster.

MOUSE—Velour, felt, or a short-pile fake fur in grey or brown is suitable for Mouse. Cut four of the "mouse ear" pieces (see Fig. 30e, on page 221); sew, turn, and attach to the puppet's head. Add large wiggle eyes, a pom-pom nose, and long whiskers.

RABBIT—A white, grey, tan, or brown velour or fake-fur fabric works well for Rabbit. Cut four of the "rabbit ear" pieces (see Fig. 30d); sew, turn, and attach to the puppet's head. Rabbit's ears may need slight stuffing and gathering when sewing them to the head. Add large wiggle eyes, a pom-pom nose, and long whiskers.

REINDEER—Brown or tan velour or a short-pile fake fur is very appropriate for Reindeer. Cut four of the "reindeer ear" pieces (see Fig. 30c); sew, turn, and attach to the puppet's head. Cut four of the "reindeer antler" pieces (see Fig. 30e) out of felt and sew together using a quarter-inch seam allowance. Do not turn these pieces—they are intended to be left unturned and stuffed slightly as is. Sew the antlers close to Reindeer's ears, being certain that they are the reverse of one another. Add large wiggle eyes and a pom-pom nose (using a large red pom-pom if you want to make Rudolph).

Details for Pointed-mouth Puppets

The construction of the ear pieces used for pointed-mouth puppets remains the same as that for rounded-mouth puppets. Here are further details for each of the following animal characters.

CROCODILE—Various shades of either light brown or green velour will work well for Crocodile. If a slightly scary creature is desired, add a row of triangular-shaped teeth cut from white felt (no pattern is included). These teeth can be attached to the puppet's mouth either when first sewing the two mouth pieces of the puppet together, or sewn by hand to the finished puppet. Sew a tongue cut from red felt to the inside fold of the puppet's mouth and large wiggle eyes on its head.

DRAGON—Any shade of green velour, felt, or short-pile fake fur is suitable for Dragon. Cut four of the "dragon horn" pieces (see Fig. 31c, on page 224) from either white or yellow felt; sew and attach to the puppet's head. Add large wiggle eyes, teeth cut from felt, and a tongue.

FOX—Felt, velour, or a short-pile fake fur is appropriate for Fox, with grey, tan, brown, or red being suitable colors. Cut four of the "fox ear" pieces (see Fig. 31c); sew, turn, and attach to the puppet's head. Add large wiggle eyes and a pom-pom nose. If desired, a row of teeth and a tongue (both cut from felt) may be sewn on.

LION—A velour or fake-fur fabric, in tan or gold, is perfect for Lion. A mane can be added either by adding a strip of a long-pile fake fur or by knotting strands of yarn into the puppet's neck. Cut four of the "cat ear" pieces (see Fig. 30c); sew, turn, and attach to the puppet's head. Add large wiggle eyes, a pom-pom nose, and whiskers.

RAT—Either velour, felt, or a very short-pile fake fur works well for Rat. Suitable colors include grey, tan, and white. Cut four of the "rat ear" pieces (see Fig. 31d, on page 225); sew, turn, and attach to the puppet's head. Add small wiggle eyes, a pom-pom nose, and long whiskers. If desired, a few sharp teeth and a tongue can be cut from felt and sewn into the puppet's mouth.

WOLF—Fake fur or velour in either brown or grey is appropriate for Wolf. Cut four of the "wolf ear" pieces (see Fig. 31d); sew, turn, and attach to the puppet's head. Add large wiggle eyes, a pom-pom nose, and a tongue cut from red felt and sewn to the inside fold of Wolf's mouth.

HAND PUPPETS

Here is a simple pattern for a hand puppet. Human characters work well as hand puppets; for that reason, this pattern features sew-on hands and a head. This way, one color or type of fabric can be used for the puppet's body while another is used for its head and hands. Fabrics which work nicely with hand puppets are velour, felt, polyester knit, and cotton. All you need to do to create a hand puppet is:

1. Place on fold of fabric and cut two of the "body" pattern (Fig. 32a). If desired, the puppet's body can be made longer merely by lengthening the bottom edge of the pattern.

2. Place on fold of fabric and cut two of the "head" pattern (Fig. 32b).

3. Cut four of the "hand" pattern (Fig. 32b). If the fabric has a distinct wrong side, be certain to reverse the pattern when cutting two of the hand pieces. Remember that the puppet's hands need to have the thumb pointing up, towards the puppet's face.

4. Sew the head to the body along the one short seam. After sewing, press these seams open.

5. Sew the hand to the ends of each arm on the puppet's body, making certain to keep the thumb of each hand pointing up. After sewing all four hands, press each seam open.

6. With the right sides of the fabric together (seams on the outside), sew the front and back of the puppet together.

7. After sewing the two pieces together, carefully clip any curved areas and turn the puppet right side out.

8. Add finishing touches for each puppet character.

To manipulate your hand puppet, place your hand into the puppet and use whichever manipulation position is most comfortable for you (see the "Puppet Manipulation" section of part 1 for further details).

For more ideas on how to make hand puppets, see appendix B. By far, one of the most workable hand puppet patterns I have ever used is Jennifer MacLennan's, which is included in her book, *Simple Puppets You Can Make*.

(Text continues on page 230.)

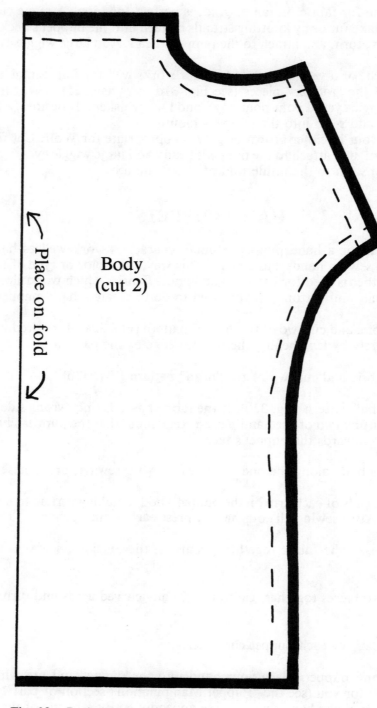

Body
(cut 2)

Place on fold

Fig. 32a. Basic hand puppet pattern

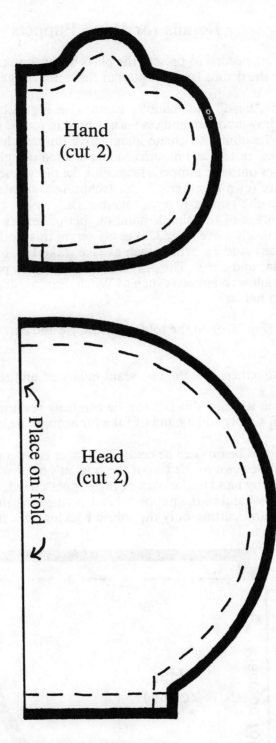

Fig. 32b. Basic hand puppet pattern

Details for Hand Puppets

All of the human characters needed to present the plays in this book can be constructed using this simple hand puppet pattern. Because the details for each human character are very similar with this type of puppet, I discuss them in broad terms.

SKIN AND FACES—The "head" and "hand" patterns (see Fig. 32b) may be cut from any color fabric. This allows the puppeteer to draw upon an endless variety of skin tones, resulting not only in a wide range of racial backgrounds, but also the ability to create imaginative human characters with green, pink, or purple flesh. Facial details such as eyes, noses, and mouths can be created using embroidery techniques or by sewing felt, pom-poms, and wiggle eyes onto the puppet's face. Fine detailing, such as embroidery, is best done before the puppet's head and body are sewn together. Simple techniques, such as adding wiggle eyes and pom-pom noses, can easily be done after the puppet is sewn together.

CLOTHING—One advantage of this simple hand puppet pattern is that you do not need to sew clothes for each character. The simple body piece (Fig. 32a) easily serves this clothing function. Fabric with stripes or prints work well for this reason. Adding details such as lace, fake fur, or other trims results in the puppet's seeming to have a distinct collar and cuffs. The only additional pattern piece I thought was necessary for the hand puppet is the "hat." This allows characters such as Witch, Santa, Elf, and Troll to wear a very simple hat. All you need to do to create a hat is:

1. Place the hat pattern (Fig. 32c) on the fold of the fabric and cut. Felt or a fake fur works best for the hat.

2. With the right sides together, sew the one seam indicated and turn right side out.

Once the puppet has been given its hair, this hat can be carefully sewn directly onto the puppet's head. For characters such as Santa or Elf, simply add a band of fake fur around the bottom of the hat and a pom-pom at the hat's tip to finish.

HAIR—Hair, mustaches, and beards can be created for your human puppet characters, using either fake fur or yarn. Pieces of yarn can be sewn to the top of the puppet's head when the two puppet pieces are sewn together. Yarn can then be sewn by hand to the back of the puppet's head, cut, and knotted securely. Pieces of fake fur can be carefully sewn by hand to the puppet's head. Remember that fake fur is always cut back from the back, using sharp scissors, and cutting only the fabric backing, not the fur.

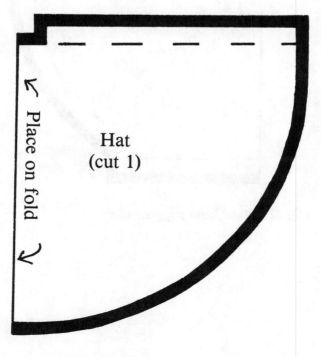

Fig. 32c. Basic hand puppet pattern

Appendix A — Resources

These are some of the companies and organizations which I have found useful as sources for books, puppets, and inspiration. The prices of the puppets are all reasonable, but several of the puppet manufacturers have specific ordering policies and may require an order of up to several hundred dollars to start an account. Please write or telephone each company or organization for more detailed information.

APPLAUSE, INC.
6101 Variel Avenue
Woodland Hills, California 91365
Telephone: 1-800-777-6990
A wide range of plush mouth and hand puppets is available, featuring both animal and human characters. A large minimum order is required to begin an account.

COUNTRY CRITTERS
217 Neosho Street
Burlington, Kansas 66839
Telephone: (316) 364-8623 or 1-800-444-9648
Offers a line of realistic hand puppets and plush toys featuring animal and barnyard characters. With a large minimum order, a discount is available.

CRAZY CRITTERS, INC.
3140 Spring Street
P.O. Box 5569
Redwood City, California 94063
Telephone: (415) 365-5253
A variety of humorous-looking mouth puppets is available, featuring human, animal, Christmas, and Biblical characters. No minimum order is required.

DAKIN, INC.
P.O. Box 7746
San Francisco, California 94120
Telephone: (415) 952-1777
A popular manufacturer of plush toys and hand and mouth puppets. Depending on the situation, non-profit and educational organizations may place large orders directly with the company.

FOLKMANIS, INC.
1219 Park Avenue
Emeryville, California 94608
Telephone: (415) 658-7677
Carries realistic hand puppets featuring animal and human characters. Schools, libraries, and other non-profit organizations may be eligible for a discount on large orders.

NANCY RENFRO STUDIOS
1117 West 9th Street
Austin, Texas 78703
Telephone: (512) 472-2140
A large array of whimsical mouth and hand puppets is available, along with books on puppetry and several portable puppet stages. Many of the books and puppets are geared toward work with special or disabled children. Orders of any quantity are welcomed.

NATIONAL ASSOCIATION FOR THE PRESERVATION AND PERPETUATION OF
     STORYTELLING (NAPPS)
P.O. Box 309
Jonesborough, Tennessee 37659
Telephone: (615) 753-2171
A nonprofit organization founded in 1975 which has been largely responsible for the recent revival of storytelling. Members receive a discount for NAPPS-sponsored institutes, conferences, and festivals; a quarterly journal; a monthly newsletter; a directory of storytellers; and a catalog of resources (tapes, records, books, etc.) available for purchase. Although not directly concerned with puppetry, NAPPS offers wonderful resource material which puppeteers will find useful.

THE PUPPETRY STORE
1525 24th S.E.
Auburn, Washington 98002
Telephone: (206) 833-8377
Offers a wide range of books, booklets, and pamphlets on all aspects of puppetry. Although affiliated with Puppeteers of America, Inc., members and nonmembers alike may request information or place orders for materials.

PUPPETEERS OF AMERICA, INC.
c/o Membership Officer
#5 Cricklewood Path
Pasadena, California 91107
This nonprofit national organization is open to both professional and amateur puppeteers. Members receive a discount for Puppeteers of America-sponsored conferences and workshops; a quarterly journal; a membership directory, and free advisory services on all aspects of puppetry.

RAGZ CREATIONS
P.O. Box 768
Decatur, Illinois 62525
Telephone: (217) 429-1208
Offers several basic mouth puppets with interchangeable eyes, noses, ears, horns, etc., allowing both adults and children to create an endless variety of imaginative puppet characters. Orders of any size are accepted.

WIZARD OF AHHS, INC.
P.O. Box 851
Pollock Pines, California 95726
Telephone: (916) 644-3524 or 1-800-331-0887
Both adult- and child-sized hand mitts are available with a wide array of attachable finger characters suitable for storytelling or finger rhymes. Also offers some hand puppets. Welcomes orders in any quantity.

Appendix B – Recommended Books on Puppetry

Here are some titles I have found helpful in my own study of puppetry. Some of them are unfortunately out of print, but may still be available through your library.

Baird, Bill. *The Art of the Puppet*. New York: Macmillan, 1965.

A lavishly illustrated history of puppetry in all its variations. Especially good for its comprehensive coverage of puppetry in other cultures. Excellent for browsing or for serious study.

Champlin, Connie. *Puppetry and Creative Dramatics in Storytelling*. Austin, Texas: Nancy Renfro Studios, 1980.

By mixing aspects of puppetry and creative dramatics, Champlin has produced a variety of activities based upon books. Topics covered include conflict, dialogue, sound effects, characterization, and mime. Liberally illustrated with black-and-white photographs and line drawings.

Champlin, Connie, and Nancy Renfro. *Storytelling with Puppets*. Chicago: American Library Association, 1985.

A very comprehensive and readable treatment of the many possible uses of puppets in storytelling. Contains some excellent patterns for puppets and useful bibliographies. Illustrated with black-and-white photographs.

Coad Canada Puppets. *Classroom Stages*. North Vancouver, British Columbia: Coad Canada Puppets, 1974.

A helpful booklet containing detailed directions for constructing several practical and compact puppet stages which are suitable for use with glove puppets, marionettes, and shadow puppets.

Condon, Camy. *Try on My Shoe: Step into Another Culture*. 1981 (available either from Lynne Jennings, 281 E. Millan Street, Chula Vista, California 92010 or The Puppetry Store (see appendix A)).

With cultural awareness as its goal, this self-published booklet contains four folktales from East Africa, Mexico, Vietnam, and the Native American tradition which have been adapted into participatory puppet presentations. Also includes a brief history of puppets, presentation tips, and directions for creating basic puppets. Illustrated by Lynne Jennings with line drawings.

Currell, David. *The Complete Book of Puppet Theatre*. New York: Barnes & Noble, 1985.

An academic examination of the history of puppetry and its uses throughout the world. Well illustrated with black-and-white photographs and line drawings.

Currell, David. *Learning with Puppets*. Boston, Massachusetts: Plays, Inc., 1980.

The emphasis here is upon puppetry in education, including puppet construction and presentation techniques, along with examples of puppetry activities. Presents some very practical and useful ideas for teachers or librarians. Illustrated with line drawings and black-and-white photographs.

Engler, Larry, and Carol Fijan. *Making Puppets Come Alive*. New York: Taplinger Publishing, 1973.

Through large black-and-white photographs and simple language, this book encourages puppeteers to become more accomplished at puppet manipulation, vocal characterization, and the creation of distinct puppet personalities. "Must" reading for every puppeteer!

Forte, Imogene. *The Puppet Factory*. Nashville, Tennessee: Incentive Publications, 1984.

Aimed at children, this is a fun collection of directions for making simple hand, mouth, finger, and paper-bag puppets from common objects. Also contains suggestions for simple stages and creative uses for puppets. Illustrated with numerous line drawings.

Hanford, Robert. *The Complete Book of Puppets & Puppeteering*. New York: Sterling, 1981.

A useful overview for the beginning puppeteer. Covers all aspects of puppet creation and play production. Especially helpful are the sections dealing with mistakes to avoid and tips from professional puppeteers. Illustrated with line drawings and black-and-white photographs.

Hunt, Tamara, and Nancy Renfro. *Celebrate: Holidays, Puppets and Creative Drama*. Austin, Texas: Nancy Renfro Studios, 1987.

Concentrates upon using puppets and creative drama with children as a way to learn about holidays from around the world. Includes patterns for simple puppets. Illustrated with line drawings and black-and-white photographs.

Hunt, Tamara, and Nancy Renfro. *Puppetry in Early Childhood Education*. Austin, Texas: Nancy Renfro Studios, 1982.

Emphasizes ways that puppets can enhance the education and development of preschool children. Includes recommended activities and simple patterns for puppets. Illustrated with line drawings and black-and-white photographs.

Keefe, Betty. *Fingerpuppet Tales: Making and Using Puppets with Folk and Fairytales*. Omaha, Nebraska: Special Literature Press, 1986.

_____. *Fingerpuppets, Fingerplays and Holidays*. Omaha, Nebraska: Special Literature Press, 1984.

Both volumes contain complete directions, patterns, stories, and follow-up activities for a variety of holiday-related and folktale-inspired finger puppets. Contain some very useful bibliographies, along with black-and-white photographs and line drawings.

Lasky, Kathryn. *Puppeteer*. New York: Macmillan, 1985.

Follows professional puppeteer Paul Vincent Davis as he mounts an elaborate production of *Aladdin and His Wonderful Lamp* at his Puppet Show Place in Boston, Massachusetts. Fascinating behind-the-scenes black-and-white photographs and an inspiring text.

Latshaw, George. *Puppetry: The Ultimate Disguise*. New York: Richards Rosen Press, 1978.

Part of the "Theatre Students" series which discusses puppetry in relation to the broader scope of theatre. Contains concise and practical information on all phases of puppetry. Illustrated with black-and-white photographs and line drawings.

Lewis, Shari, and Lilliam Oppenheimer. *Folding Paper Puppets*. Briarcliff Manor, New York: Stein & Day, 1962.

Based upon simple origami techniques, contains complete instructions for making over a dozen basic puppets by folding paper. Clear directions accompanied by diagrams and black-and-white photographs. A fun variation of puppet construction for older children.

MacLennan, Jennifer. *Simple Puppets You Can Make.* New York: Sterling, 1988.

Complete patterns and instructions to make a wide variety of finger, mouth, and hand puppets featuring human and animal characters. Clear directions accompanied by line drawings and some color photographs. Essential for anyone wanting to create their own puppets.

Mehrens, Gloria, and Karen Wick. *Bagging It with Puppets.* Belmont, California: Fearon/David S. Lake Publishers, 1988.

Reproducible patterns and directions for making a variety of both human and animal puppets from paper bags. An added feature is that each puppet represents an animal or person whose name corresponds to a letter of the alphabet. Accompanied by line drawings.

Morgan, Kathleen, JoEllen Moore, and Joy Evans. *Animal Puppets.* Monterey, California: Evan-Moor, 1988.

Directions for creating a variety of simple animal mouth puppets from just one simple folded piece of paper. Clear diagrams and directions make this a useful resource when working with children.

Nichols, Judy. *Storytimes for Two-Year-Olds.* Chicago: American Library Association, 1987.

A comprehensive guide to planning, promoting, and presenting story programs for this age group. Also includes instructions for making simple puppets, puppet stages, and an excellent bibliography. Illustrated with black-and-white photographs and line drawings.

Painter, William M. *Musical Story Hours: Using Music with Storytelling and Puppetry.* Hamden, Connecticut: The Shoe String Press, 1989.

An interesting collection of suggestions for pairing musical pieces with picture books and puppet presentations, resulting in unique storytelling experiences. Divided into general themes, such as bears, tall tales, holidays, dance, etc.

Pittman, Jeanne W. *Fanciful Furry Finger Friends.* San Diego, California: Pittman Puppet Productions, 1983.

A useful booklet filled with detailed patterns and directions for numerous animal finger puppets. Easy-to-follow instructions illustrated with line drawings of the finished puppets.

Renfro, Nancy. *A Puppet Corner in Every Library.* Austin, Texas: Nancy Renfro Studios, 1978.

Written especially for librarians, this book offers practical ideas for the creation, circulation, and use of puppets in a library setting. Illustrated with black-and-white photographs and line drawings.

Renfro, Nancy. *Puppet Shows Made Easy!* Austin, Texas: Nancy Renfro Studies, 1984.

A guide for planning and presenting puppet plays which is ideal for the beginning puppeteer. Illustrated with line drawings and black-and-white photographs.

Renfro, Nancy. *Puppetry and the Art of Story Creation.* Austin, Texas: Nancy Renfro Studios, 1979.

A step-by-step examination of what makes a successful puppet play. Excellent ideas for creative scripts which emphasize the puppeteer's use of imagination. Illustrated with line drawings.

Renfro, Nancy, and Beverly Armstrong. *Make Amazing Puppets.* Santa Barbara, California: The Learning Works, 1979.

This thin booklet contains a wealth of ideas and instructions for making puppets from scrap items such as cups, envelopes, paper plates, plastic bottles, and boxes. Ideal when planning workshops on puppet creation for children or adults. Well illustrated with line drawings.

Renfro, Nancy, and Nancy Frazier. *Imagination: At Play with Puppets and Creative Drama*. Austin, Texas: Nancy Renfro Studios, 1987.

A variety of everyday objects plus a little imagination results in some of the creative, often wacky puppets described here. Also concentrates upon using music, art, and movement in the creative process with children.

Ross, Laura. *Hand Puppets and How to Make Them*. New York: Lothrop, Lee & Shepard, 1969.

A basic guide to creating all types of glove puppets, from paper-bag puppets to papier-mâché. Very useful when constructing puppets with children. Illustrated with black-and-white photographs.

Sims, Judy. *Puppets for Dreaming and Scheming: A Puppet Source Book*. Santa Barbara, California: The Learning Works, 1988.

An excellent guide for adults working with children. Includes directions for easy-to-construct mouth, stick, finger, and shadow puppets and marionettes. Also includes creative uses for puppets and tips on manipulation, puppet voices, and staging. Well illustrated with Beverly Armstrong's comic line drawings.

Stangl, Jean. *Fingerlings: Finger Puppet Fun for Little Ones*. Belmont, California: Fearon/David S. Lake Publishers, 1986.

Directions for easy-to-make finger puppets from cloth, paper, and gloves are included, along with simple stages and storage ideas for finger puppets. Accompanied by original rhymes and stories for these "fingerlings." Illustrated with line drawings.

Tichenor, Tom. *Tom Tichenor's Puppets*. Nashville, Tennessee: Abingdon Press, 1971.

Based upon his experiences as a puppeteer for library storytimes and other occasions, Tichenor shares his philosophy of puppetry. Included are useful directions for making glove puppets, as well as several puppet scripts which advanced puppeteers will enjoy presenting.

Verkest, Susan. *Crocheting Storybook Hand Puppets*. New York: Dover, 1981.

Directions for crocheting simple hand puppets are included, featuring characters from Mother Goose rhymes and traditional folk tales. Many of the patterns will need to be adapted in order to create puppets suitable for puppet play presentation. Illustrated with black-and-white and color photographs.

Williams, DeAtna A. *Paper-bag Puppets*. Belmont, California: David S. Lake Publishers, 1966.

A collection of reproducible patterns for numerous paper-bag puppets, featuring animal and holiday characters. Illustrated with line drawings and black-and-white photographs.

Wright, Lyndie. *Puppets*. New York: Franklin Watts, 1989.

An excellent source for workable puppet-making ideas which children can easily use. Discusses how to construct simple puppets using papier-mâché, fabric, and styrofoam. Large color photographs accompany the clear directions.